BE HUNTED!

12 Secrets to Getting on the Headhunter's Radar Screen

SMOOCH S. REYNOLDS

John Wiley & Sons, Inc.

New York ■ Chichester ■ Weinheim ■ Brisbane ■ Singapore ■ Toronto

Published by John Wiley & Sons, Inc.

Published simultaneously in Canada.

This publication is designed to provide accurate and authoritative
information in regard to the subject matter covered. It is sold
with the understanding that the publisher is not engaged in
rendering professional services. If professional advice or other
expert assistance is required, the services of a competent
professional person should be sought.

Library of Congress Cataloging-in-Publication Data:

Reynolds, Smooch S.
    Be Hunted! 12 secrets to getting on the headhunter's radar screen /
Smooch S. Reynolds.
        p. cm.
    Includes bibliographical references and index.
    ISBN 0-471-41074-8 (pbk. : alk. paper)
    1. Executive search firms. 2. Career development. 3. Executives—
Recruiting. I. Title.

HF5549.5R44 R49 2001
650.1'4'088658—dc21   2001026073

Printed in the United States of America.

10 9 8 7 6 5 4 3 2 1

This book is dedicated wholly to Renard, Sweet Pea, Sugar Plum, and Slugger, who are the center of my life. The countless hours they have spent sending their love and support to me throughout my travels as a headhunter are priceless.

In addition, I must acknowledge my father Mike N. Repovich, whose neverending drive and encouragement to reach beyond all expectations will always be a part of my soul ... as will the many memories I have of his tough exterior and soft heart.

Contents

Contents

Foreword

Scott A. Scanlon

Chairman and Chief Executive
Hunt-Scanlon Advisors

In today's competitive hiring market, it is critical for candidates to understand the highly complex rules of job transition and career management before jumping into the game of finding a new job. Candidates who take a knee-jerk approach to their job search and interview process are certain to be pushed to the sidelines by executive recruiters, hiring executives, and more astute job seekers who understand how to navigate the job search process and their career. When it comes to finding your next job, or launching a new career, it can be a cruel world out there. You must be on your toes, know the ropes, and be as sophisticated as your competition is likely to be. To get there, you need to read this book—twice! It has everything you need to know to get that elusive offer that can change your life.

In *Be Hunted! 12 Secrets to Getting on the Headhunter's Radar Screen,* Smooch S. Reynolds has written the quintessential guide to help any job seeker become a sophisticated twenty-first-century candidate. This book provides candidates with a nuts-and-bolts primer and empowers them to take full advantage of how to work with executive search professionals and hiring authorities—all the while maximizing their options in the process. Because today's marketplace can be a minefield for the uninformed job seeker, this book is a must-read for anyone undergoing career change and transition.

In addition to providing job-search tips and lessons learned from one of the nation's top recruiters, *Be Hunted!* also serves as a timeless code of conduct for every level of job seeker—a behavioral guide that all twenty-first-century job candidates need to follow as they begin the rite of passage from one job to the next or from one career to another.

Of all the books currently available on the topic of finding your next job, this book stands out because of its author. Smooch is the founder, president, and CEO of a leading executive search firm in Pasadena, California, who specializes in finding top-flight talent for communications, marketing, and investor relations functions within world-class companies. I've known Smooch for as many years as I've had my business—13 years now!—and I have had the pleasure of getting to know her over the course of that time on both a professional and personal level. From that experience, I can say unequivocally that Smooch S. Reynolds is one of the finest executive recruiters I have ever met. Whatever you take away from this book, keep in mind some of the fundamental rules that Smooch S. Reynolds follows, and why I think she has been so successful in getting to the top of her game: She abides by a stringent code of ethics in managing her business; she builds relationships with clients, candidates, and professional acquaintances with a tremendous amount of mutual respect; and, she approaches her profession valuing raw intellect, intuitive street smarts, and myriad intangible qualities that represent success.

Follow these fundamentals, and you'll find your next job or new career opportunity before you know it.

This is a timely book on executive recruiting and job hunting. As the search industry's "watchdog," I have tracked this profession now for over a decade. During that time I have seen the recruiting business transform itself from a cottage industry to the highly respected profession that it is today. The fact is it's more difficult to find a job today without the assistance of a good executive recruiter. So take the time to read what Smooch has to say; it *will* change your life!

Preface

I've long wondered how people have navigated their careers when the marketplace has had such a dearth of genuine information that can empower professionals to take ownership of their careers. Yes, there are hundreds of how-to books about writing resumes and dressing for success and interviewing techniques. But do they really hit you right between the eyes to the degree that you have a sudden epiphany about how to navigate your career successfully? Probably not.

It never fails that when I am giving a speech, someone in the audience raises his or her hand and mentions the proverbial "they"—*they* say this and *they* say that. Who are the "theys" in society making these ridiculous statements and setting these absurd rules about career navigation? I certainly haven't met them. Have you?

In this book, I hope to impart nearly every bit of wisdom and knowledge that races through my mind 24/7. Endless thoughts and ideas, facts, and realities about the executive search profession that no one ... I guarantee you ... has ever mentioned to you in college or during the years of your career. It's all about getting a reality check about career navigation and putting yourself on an equal footing with the executive search community and the hiring corporations.

So what the heck do you do with a headhunter anyway?

Stripping the Secrets from the Executive Search Profession

Behind the Mahogany Doors

Executive recruiter. Just what does that enigmatic term mean? There is no dictionary definition. Yet ask just about anyone what an executive recruiter does, and for many the term will conjure up images of trips on private jets, three-martini lunches, expensively tailored suits, and conversations in hushed tones behind heavy, mahogany doors. In the eyes of many, it represents a high-level, high-life, clandestine world.

Although the imagination might run wild speculating how an executive recruiter spends her professional life, much of what lies behind those mahogany doors must remain shrouded in mystery owing to the nature of the vocation. Confidentiality is at the very core of a successful executive search or recruiter's practice.

1

In the search process, headhunters learn about candidates' backgrounds and hold secret the many intimate details of their professional and personal lives. Similarly, the search professional also learns corporate and trade secrets of his client companies and of their executives. Holding these details in confidence is critical for a headhunter to survive in the executive search field. Any executive recruiter who violates the trust of a candidate or a client soon will be on the street seeking his next job.

Yet opening those doors to share some of what really goes on behind them, while at the same time not compromising anyone's confidences, can be tricky in order to bring an understanding of how it all works to those seeking jobs—the candidates—as well as to those seeking to fill jobs—the hiring executives. By sharing my insights into some of those secrets, real or perceived, it is my hope that you will gain a better understanding of the profession. This, in turn, will lead to candidates being able to navigate more successful and fulfilling careers, hiring executives finding better candidates, and executive recruiters bringing both more success stories. These fundamentals should be the goals for any headhunter who runs a successful operation. Otherwise, why would they exist? What is their raison d'être?

What Is a Recruiter?

The foremost "secret" or mystery for many in the job search process is gaining an understanding of what a recruiter is, what her role is in the search process, and how someone utilizes a recruiter's services. Unless you have reached a certain point in your career and have interfaced with an executive recruiter or otherwise have had direct contact with one—such as having a relative or friend with that occupation—you may go through life never knowing, or needing to know, what someone with that title actually does for a living. Believe it or not, it truly remains a mystery for many.

When I began my career in executive search in the mid-1980s, I experienced how few people really understood what an executive recruiter did. Although some who had worked with a recruiter obviously knew what that profession entailed—that fundamentally, executive recruiters recruit executives for jobs—others expressed a vague notion of what the profession was all about. Here's how a conversation about my occupation might unfold. "What do you do?" the inquirer would ask. "I'm an executive recruiter," I would respond proudly. The inquirer would look askance and say, "Oh. You're one of those. A headhunter." Then she might smirk, "What exactly does a headhunter do—hunt heads?" A guffaw would usually follow.

I've now become accustomed to this response by the uninitiated. And over the years, I have actually come to embrace the term *headhunter* and have accepted the image some might have of me—that of a clandestine voodoo priestess wielding a tomahawk. It generally goes along with the territory. But this type of response also has prompted me to recognize that even those who have dealt with a headhunter do not have a solid understanding of what we do! Or they might think they know, but in reality they don't, as they do not have the information they need to be able to determine if a recruiter is of a certain caliber.

So what does an executive recruiter really do? In subsequent chapters, we will delve into the details of answering this question. However, simply stated, an executive recruiter—or headhunter, in the vernacular—is a professional who represents a company or organization as an independent, third-party, or in-house entity and seeks to recruit candidates to fill a particular position or positions within a company. According to Hunt-Scanlon Advisors, publishers of resources for executive recruiters, human resource professionals, and job seekers, there are approximately eight thousand executive recruitment professionals and eighteen hundred search firms worldwide, and these numbers are growing at a rapid rate. Based on that statistic alone, there certainly is clear evidence that these individuals are known entities to a segment of the population and serve an important and needed function.

The profession is relatively new, dating back to the post–World War II era when America returned to a prosperous peacetime economy during the 1950s and 1960s. This prosperity resulted in a tight labor market and spawned a need for companies to hire third parties to scour the landscape for talent at competing companies, and thus executive recruiters and an industry were born. Over the years, recruiters have gained increasing credibility and importance in bringing top talent to corporate America. They truly have become the gatekeepers to the nation's top jobs.

Backgrounds of Recruiters—
Know with Whom You Are Dealing

When you work with a recruiter, it is critical that you know who is sitting across the desk from you. After all, besides your spouse, family members, close friends, physicians, and possibly mortgage brokers and insurance agents, there are few other individuals with whom you will share some of the most intimate details of your life. As I mentioned earlier, these are some of the secrets that a recruiter needs to know about you and should be held in confidence. Although the recruiter primarily will be interested in the professional side of your life, he or she also will need to learn about your reasons for wanting to seek a new position, and some of those reasons might be of a highly personal nature to you.

Some candidates may have cause to leave their job stemming directly from changes at the company that employs them, for example, a downsizing, an acquisition, or a restructuring. Or perhaps a new chief executive officer (CEO) comes on board and wants to bring in members of his or her own team, and that leaves you out on the street. These are all very typical reasons a candidate launches a job search.

However, some reasons why candidates choose to find a new position are due to changes in their personal life—an elderly parent in another state who needs care, better special educational options for their children, a spouse's new position with an out-of-state company, a divorce, a disability, a desire to live closer to the beach. There are myriad personal reasons for wanting to leave a job.

You may be inclined to want to hide those personal details, as the real reason for wanting to leave a job might be embarrassing to you, or you might think you are divulging too much intimate detail to the search professional. Although you do not want to bare your soul to the recruiter, it *is* in your best interest to share all pertinent facts with the recruiter so that she can do her best in finding the optimal opportunity for you. Ideally, that will be a new position that meets all of your needs, both professional and personal. However, be certain you know with whom you are dealing and that this personal information will be held in confidence by the recruiter and not shared with others whom she might meet at the local watering hole. We'll explore in Chapter 6 more concerning how much information about your personal life is appropriate to share with the recruiter.

Choosing a Recruiter

How do you select a recruiter? The best way is to conduct thorough research about the reputation of his firm as well as securing information on the individual recruiter's background and character. It is critical that you know in whose hands you are putting your future. You must have complete trust and confidence in the ability of the recruiter who is either going to bring you your next best career step or waste your time and possibly even misrepresent you to a potential employer and ruin your chances of securing an interview.

I'll offer more insights into how best to conduct research into the backgrounds of executive search professionals and their firms in Chapter 3. However, as a rule of thumb you may want to begin by asking a trusted colleague or mentor whom they might know and recommend in the executive search profession. If you are a member of a professional organization, inquire among fellow members, ask the chapter president, or seek out other resources within the organization. You may also contact editors of executive recruiter news publications, or you may tap into online resources for search firms' own Web sites or use the myriad search engines for news and information on the firm. If the firm provides a list of clients on its site, pick up the phone, contact one of the clients, and speak with the human resource department about their impression of the firm.

There are many ways to accomplish learning more about the reputation of a firm and its recruiters. But whatever you do, just be sure to take this critical step to learn more about whom you are entrusting with your future and your confidences.

No Academic Degree in Executive Recruiting

No degree in executive recruiting exists in academic curricula today. There is no Ph.D. in headhunting. Although certain expected and earned credentials may go along with being a search professional, virtually anyone can hang a shingle and suddenly announce that she has become an executive recruiter. There are no rigorous intellectual tests to pass, no certificates required, no executive review boards with whom to pass muster, and no scholars ensuring that lofty tomes have been read and committed to memory before someone can become a search professional. There will be no framed board certification hanging on a recruiter's wall that will give you the confidence or assurance that the person holding the key to your future, to your next best career step, to the job you might have for the rest of your life, is a bright, capable and—most importantly—reputable individual. Even your garage mechanic is usually required to be certified, but not executive recruiters. In short, there is no one common educational requirement that an executive recruiter must have to practice the profession. The thought is a little scary.

However, hope is not lost in learning how to evaluate an executive recruiter's experience and background before you commit to working with one. There are some common threads among the backgrounds of recruitment professionals that you will discover in your research and that should serve as assurance to you that you are dealing with a reputable individual or firm. Let's take a glimpse at the experience and backgrounds of some of the pioneers, leading executives, and successful newcomers in the profession, as well as the firms for which they work, and you can judge for yourself what commonality you might find among them.

Gerard (Gerry) R. Roche. Mr. Roche is chairman of the international search firm of Heidrick & Struggles. The retained firm specializes in conducting high-level positions such as CEO, chief financial officer (CFO), and director. Mr. Roche has more than thirty years of experience in executive search. He has a B.S. from the University of Scranton, an M.B.A. from New York University, and an honorary Doctor of Laws degree from the University of Scranton.

Windle B. Priem. Mr. Priem is vice chairman and chief operating officer (COO) of Korn/Ferry International. The retained firm specializes in senior-level executive placements worldwide. Mr. Priem has a B.S. from Worcester Polytechnic Institute and an M.B.A. from Babson Institute of Business Administration.

Dennis C. Carey. Dr. Carey is vice chairman of Spencer Stuart, U.S., and comanaging director of the U.S. board services practice of Spencer Stuart. The retained firm specializes in conducting search for senior-level executives and board directors worldwide. Dr. Carey holds a Ph.D. in finance and administration from the University of Maryland and was a postdoctoral fellow at Harvard University.

7

David Beirne. Mr. Beirne is a general partner of Benchmark
Capital and was a founding partner of Ramsey/Beirne
Associates. Mr. Beirne specializes in senior-level retained
executive search for the high-technology industry. He
holds a B.S. from Bryant College.

Charles W. Sweet. Mr. Sweet is president of A.T. Kearney
Executive Search, the global executive recruiting division of A.T. Kearney, Inc., a wholly owned subsidiary
of EDS. Mr. Sweet has a B.A. in English and econom-
ics from Hamilton College and an M.B.A. in personnel and finance from the University of Chicago.

And a bit about my background:

Smooch S. Reynolds—Ms. Reynolds is founder, president, and CEO of The Repovich-Reynolds Group, a
retained executive search firm specializing in placing
senior-level executives in the investor relations, communications, and marketing disciplines worldwide.
Ms. Reynolds has a B.A. in broadcast journalism from
the University of Southern California.

Granted, these are brief biographical summaries, but certain commonalities pop out even in short paragraphs, such
as the scope of these individuals' search practice being "international," "global," and "worldwide." It is quickly evident that
these professionals must have reached certain accomplishments to have achieved a level of work so broad in geo-
graphical scope. Another common thread you'll observe is the
fact that the firm they manage or by which they are employed
is a *retained* search firm. That means a client retains, or contracts with, the firm to conduct an exclusive search on the
client company's behalf. (We'll explore more about what that
term encompasses in subsequent chapters.) And each has a
college education. Although some have bachelor's degrees in
English and some in finance and others have received their
doctoral degree, all of these professionals have earned a four-
year degree from an accredited college or university. This

education has given them the fundamentals and foundation from which to build a career in just about any profession.

However, their diverse educational backgrounds also underscores the fact that none of these individuals has majored in the same subject in college, which supports my earlier discussion that there is no degree in executive recruiting. To become a successful executive recruiter, one must possess broad skills, both tangible and intangible. Some of the tangible attributes, such as education; career progression; size, scope, and reputation of the company with which he has worked prior to entering the search field; and years of experience, can be easy to assess. Other intangible attributes you would want the recruiter to possess are more difficult to gauge. And it is imperative that you feel comfortable with the recruiter's personal qualities, particularly because the recruiter will be assessing you for the very same thing—your attributes beyond professional accomplishments.

Beyond the College Degree

What else can you look for in the backgrounds of a recruiter as you strive to learn more about the person to whom you hand the key to your future? Most executive recruiters' backgrounds are just as diverse as the major that she had chosen in college. One doesn't usually land a job as a headhunter directly out of college. Many recruiters pursue this line of work as a second career, typically after having held high-level management jobs where they have gained hands-on knowledge of the inner workings of a corporation as well as building contacts in a specific industry or function. The recruiter can then leverage both the knowledge she has gained in business as well as the contacts developed and nurtured over the years to build a successful practice.

Some recruiters may join a large executive search firm in a support-level role, such as a researcher, and move up to a search position. However, this experience is not as broad as the recruiters who have spent years in the trenches of the corporate world. A successful recruiter should have developed solid life skills gained through facing numerous challenges and solving real-life situations encountered in a role with a corporation, government entity, or other such organization. Check his background. Did the recruiter have a successful career as a senior-level manager in a Fortune 25 company? Or was he a lawyer? An entrepreneur? A human resource professional? In your research did you find that the recruiter failed in another career and now is positioning himself as an expert in the recruiting field? These are important factors to know about a search professional.

In short, you want to feel that the headhunter with whom you are working is not only qualified to assess your skills and experience but also has the good judgment to assess your own intangible skills. Unless the recruiter has some kind of inborn psychic ability that might be seen on a "believe it or not" type of TV program, only years of experience can enable the recruiter to have the expertise, wisdom, maturity, and judgment to assess *your* intangible attributes. *Nothing* can take the place of these years of experience to equip a professional with this ability.

However, sometimes even years of experience doesn't guarantee the recruiter will have these abilities. It is ultimately up to you to be able to discern whether or not the recruiter can size you up and portray your skills and intangible attributes accurately to a client for a position she is seeking to fill. You must be comfortable with the gut feeling you have about this individual. I can only give you some guidelines to follow. The responsibility to investigate and the process by which you do so are in your hands. But, again, if you conduct adequate research into the depth of experience and integrity of the recruiter and check her references, you should be able to determine if the headhunter is a capable professional whom you can trust.

A Week in the Life of an Executive Recruiter

Now, about those three-martini lunches that I mentioned at the beginning of this chapter. Because so much of the work a recruiter does is immersed in closely guarded secrecy "behind the mahogany doors," you might be inclined to concoct an image of recruiters' high-flying ways. After all, what *are* they doing behind those doors anyway? Just who are those people who are assessing me and determining if I make the grade for what could be the best job of my life—my next best career step? What do they do all day long? Or, if you are the client and the ultimate hiring authority who usually foots the bill for these headhunting activities, you may have a tremendous interest in just what's happening in those high-rent district office suites. What are the realities of the life of an executive recruiter?

Do you want to know a secret? Headhunting is not a leisure-time sport. It is not a pastime filled with days spent teeing off at private golf resorts or lounging, cocktail in hand, on a wide, white beach while chatting on a cell phone. It is not about loading skis into a helicopter destined for a powder-covered peak in search of the perfect run and—oh, by the way, while I'm up there, I might make a call or two to the client and a candidate to discuss the multimillion-dollar compensation for a dream job I'm seeking to fill. Quite the contrary.

An executive recruiter's life takes an incredible amount of stamina; it requires superb judgment, counseling, and multi-tasking skills and superior stress management abilities. One must have the stomach to handle tough competition, and long hours and frequent travel are a given—in an attempt to compete for talent on behalf of our clients who rely on us to *exceed* their staffing desires and expectations.

The reality? Recruiting can be a tremendously satisfying career, and it continues to be for me as well as for the professionals at my firm. So let me take this opportunity to dispel the rumors of the high-flying lifestyle of the executive recruiter by sharing with you what my typical workweek is like. These experiences represent a compilation of those I've had on the road in recent years as an executive recruiter.

Sunday: After spending time with the family and hosting a noon birthday party for 20 fourth graders, review the day's

11

newspapers and weekly journals and pack for a business trip to four cities in three days. Ensure batteries on laptop and cell phone are charged. Host an early evening dinner for a local client and her spouse and advise on an issue she's been faced with in her own career.

Arrive at the airport for an 11 P.M. red-eye flight from the West Coast to Ft. Lauderdale, Florida. At the airport, learn that the plane has been delayed an hour due to bad weather in the Gulf of Mexico. Use the time to begin writing a candidate profile and leave messages for colleagues to retrieve in the morning. The weather clears, the plane takes off, and the pilot says he can make up the lost time.

On the plane, spend a few hours of rare undisturbed time reading business publications and mail, writing reports, and thanking fate for the empty seat beside me ensuring that my confidential paperwork will not be seen by any fellow travelers.

Sleep three hours prior to landing.

Monday: Land in Ft. Lauderdale at 6:30 A.M. in 85-degree, 90-percent-humidity weather. Check into hotel, freshen up, and take a cab to an office park for a 9 A.M. meeting with a new dot-com client. Counsel him on the communications and investor relations department he is seeking to build and the type of professional he wants to lead it. Determine structure of the department, staffing needs, compensation packages, and process of the search. Secure contract signatures and tour the operation. Make plans to return for full due-diligence with other members of senior management.

Take a cab at 11:30 A.M. to the hotel and check in with my West Coast—based headquarters; return calls, read and return e-mail messages. Touch base with myriad clients and candidates. Check out of hotel and head to airport for the next portion of my trip to New York City. While at the airport, hand-write and send thank-you note to my Florida client, thanking him for the opportunity to serve as his search firm of record. Take time on the plane to review notes on candidate panel for New York City–based health care client, ensuring that no names are visible to seatmate or other passersby.

Arrive in New York City, check into hotel, return calls, check and return e-mail messages, and prepare for dinner interview with a candidate from a major pharmaceutical company. She appears to be a strong candidate for a senior-level marketing role in Los Angeles but needs to consider the relocation implications of leaving an elderly parent. Will likely pass on the opportunity. She is, however, interested in a marketing position in Michigan she saw posted on our firm's Web site. Qualify her for this role.

Return to room. Call the office and counsel one of my staff recruiters through issues she's having negotiating a candidate's offer. Check all messages and return them. Begin writing position descriptions for the Ft. Lauderdale client's opportunities. Call home. Review annual report of a history-making biotech client.

Sleep five hours.

Tuesday: Awake at 4 A.M. and prepare for day. Include a brisk workout in the hotel's facility and a scan of the daily papers. At 7 A.M., have breakfast with a candidate for a senior vice president of communications position with a recently reengineered multibillion-dollar technology company based in Dallas. He's qualified and interested, and the cultural fit is spot on. Schedule a follow-up phone call to gather additional material for his candidate profile documents. Meet a candidate at 8:30 A.M. whose wife recently accepted a position in the Portland area and is himself interested in learning about potential opportunities there. Discuss his qualifications for searches we are conducting for a world-renowned apparel manufacturer in the area. He appears to be highly qualified for one of the positions—a courtesy interview turns into a likely contender for the opportunity. Return to room for client conference call.

Meet the health care client for lunch and review the semifinalist candidate panel with the search committee.

Counsel client on an "off-spec" candidate whose technical experience may not be a one-for-one match of the requirements of the position but whose intangible attributes—high energy, positive mind-set, and history of rock-solid judgment calls—make him a strong contender. Client responds favorably and chooses to meet him. Wrap up discussions and select two other candidates for first-round interviews. Return to hotel for late checkout.

Go to airport for trip to Chicago. Departure delayed due to lack of available terminal docking facility for arriving flight. Contact semifinalist candidates for health care search and advise those who were selected for first-round interviews. They are delighted.

Plane docks and is cleaned, and we take off for Chicago. Scan newspapers and business publications. Use airline phone to check in with the office. In guarded tones, ask administrative assistant to schedule conference calls with two clients. Arrive in Chicago to an unexpected heavy rain. Find micro-umbrella in suitcase side compartment. Return calls en route to hotel. Check in and inquire as to the father of the doorman's health. Freshen up for dinner and return e-mail messages.

Meet candidate for dinner. She is interested in a senior-level investor relations management position with a specialty chemical company client based in St. Louis, but she has a special-needs child and is concerned about taking him out of his current school. Immediately following, meet a candidate for a director of public relations position with a start-up telecommunications company in New Jersey. He has been with the same company for a number of years, and although this position appears to be an attractive career step, he's hesitant to give up the comfortable role he's grown into for a leadership post at a start-up. Low risk-taking threshold. Not a good cultural fit.

Return to room. Check messages, return several calls and e-mails. Check in at office and at home. All's well. Review literature of major financial services company for new business meeting in the morning. Leaf through a consumer magazine.

Sleep six hours. (What a luxury!)

Wednesday: Have room service deliver breakfast and scan the morning newspapers. Complete a scheduled 20-minute potential candidate courtesy call. Complete reference checking for finalist candidate who will serve as chief investor relations officer for a major consumer products company. Head over to the financial services company for new business meeting with three key executives. Present firm's credentials. Perceive that all goes well; competing with two other firms. Wrap up meeting and make mental note to check with a trusted confidante for a reference to give this potential client. Return to hotel and take car to airport for flight to Dallas. Bad weather grounds all planes for an hour. Grab a salad at the terminal and check in with office. Storm passes, and planes are cleared for takeoff.

Arrive in Dallas for late-afternoon meeting with multi-billion-dollar high-technology client at headquarters, followed by dinner. Review progress of search to date for head of communications for an organization of 100 professionals worldwide and its five direct reports. Client is pleased. Return to airport for return flight to West Coast—and home. Plane arrives with no delays!

Thursday: Conduct 6 A.M. (West Coast time)–9 A.M. (East Coast time) telephone interview with candidate for one of the Dallas-based, high-technology company positions. Candidate's credentials are flawless. Make plans to schedule in-person meeting as soon as possible. Time is critical as he has another offer percolating. Scan newspapers. Enjoy breakfast with family. Head for office for a full day of meetings, both telephone and in person.

Hold staff meeting and discuss status of searches with recruitment team. Welcome new recruiter and ensure she is receiving all new orientation information. Celebrate three-year anniversary of another recruiter. For next three hours, conduct series of telephone interviews in back-to-back half-hour increments for two clients in two different locations and industries. As last interview wraps up, candidate from Dallas who was unavailable the day before when I passed through the city arrives for in-person lunch interview. Before greeting her, work with recruiter in office on counseling client through the experience level of candidate needed for a position. Conduct lunch interview at local restaurant. Candidate is interested in expanding her expertise in senior-level internal communications into a broader communications role with a publicly traded, multibillion-dollar retail client with whom we have an assignment. The career path for the position presents that option. She is interested and qualified.

Return to office to meet with recruiters and brainstorm strategy for identifying candidates for a leading Los Angeles–based office-supplies manufacturing and distributing company. Company wants to recruit locally. Take a call from a finalist candidate who is about to accept an offer with a Los Angeles–based dot-com company whose spouse is getting cold feet about relocating from the East Coast. Schedule call with the two of them and arrange for meeting with relocation specialist. Suggest a few neighborhoods to tour. Make plans to meet the relocation specialist and the couple to discuss options.

Meet with marketing team to discuss presentation to a professional association's global annual conference. Complete half-hour phone interview with candidate for a head of advertising and branding position with a Silicon Valley–based, Fortune 10 high-technology company. Spend remainder of day editing candidate presentation materials. That evening, attend a board meeting of local charitable organization.

Friday: Scan newspapers and business publications. Conduct a 6 A.M. new business conference call with one of the world's largest issuers of credit cards and marketer consumer lending products on the East Coast for two senior-level communications positions. Spend the morning making "touch base" calls to contacts nurtured over the years, as well as conducting outreach to new contacts. Lunch at desk drafting an op-ed piece for a national media publication. Meet with marketing department to prepare for an interview on CNN to be taped live. Hold an afternoon conference call with the CFO of the nation's largest home furniture manufacturer based in the Midwest; negotiate compensation package and discuss relocation issues for finalist vice president of investor relations candidate. Meet with administrative staff to review appointments and plans for the following week. Meet family for dinner.

Saturday: Review daily newspaper and catch up on myriad publications—business and executive search trade newsletters, both print and online. Read mail and resumes. Conduct phone interview with candidate at her home as during the weekdays she has no privacy at the high-technology firm where she works. She's a solid match for an investor relations position with a Washington, D.C.–based biotech company. Spend the rest of the day and night enjoying family time. Breathe.

So, after reviewing my typical workweek, did you see any opportunities to eke out time for a three-martini lunch? Not in this lifetime. Business *is* conducted over meals as a part of the search process and this is part of getting to know clients and candidates. However, martinis and careless downtime are not part of this process. One needs a clear head in order to provide strategic counsel to clients ranging from pre-initial-public-offer (IPO) to multibillion-dollar corporations and to properly assess a candidate's abilities and experience for some of the top jobs in the world. One doesn't do this while in a haze—you need a sharp, clear mind to be highly effective on behalf of both clients and candidates.

As for the jet-setting lifestyle, our business is one that requires in-person meetings with clients and candidates, and this necessitates frequent air travel. Although video conferencing and interviewing has its place in the search profession, in-person meetings are still critical in my opinion and always will be. How can one accurately assess demeanor and leadership skills watching a video monitor? However, for professionals whose work does not require him to be in a high-visibility leadership role, video interviewing may serve its purpose quite well. It might be an appropriate method to get to know a brilliant scientist who is typically locked behind the stainless-steel doors of his or her laboratory inventing the latest microchip technology or deciphering genetic code. That type of work does not require the dynamic, interpersonal skills needed in a chief marketing officer of a multibillion-dollar consumer product company. It's all very subjective. I will discuss this topic in more depth in a later chapter on interviewing skills.

What other secrets lie behind the mahogany doors? I'll share more with you throughout this book. But some things will remain just that—a secret. As I mentioned at the beginning of this chapter, that's what headhunting is all about—confidentiality and trust. Someone who is incapable of preserving that trust will not last long in this profession. So, with the knowledge that all is not privy to you, I'll now open the doors a little wider as I share the innermost secrets of the executive search profession.

———

Secret: Mystery solved—a recruiter *is* a headhunter. Yes, I used that utterly distasteful word that the executive search industry frowns upon—*headhunter.* However, stop and think about what we're paid to do—be on the hunt for people. The term makes perfect sense to me!

CHAPTER **2**

Types of Recruiters and Firms—In-House, Retained, Contingency, and Internet

All Recruiters Are Not Created Equal

Some headhunters would like you to believe that all recruiters are created equal. Let me share a secret with you: *They're not.* And that's a secret that is closely guarded by headhunters who lack the integrity and professionalism of their counterparts who are worthy of and have earned the right to be called an executive recruiter. It is critical for you to understand this as you navigate your career. Not all recruiters have the same experience and qualifications, the same method of recruiting, or the same ethics about how to recruit candidates and manage a search process. Just as we established in the first chapter that there are some similarities in the backgrounds of professional recruiters, there also are vast differences. I reiterate—these differences are *critical* for you to understand as you conduct your job search and entrust individuals with both your professional *and* personal destinies. You want to know as much as possible about the person who will be assessing your background for what could be the career opportunity of your life.

In today's marketplace, there are basically four types of recruiters and/or methods of recruiting: the *in-house recruiter*, who is a staff member of a company and fills positions within that organization; the *retained search firm*, which is retained or contracted by a company to fill a specific position/positions on an exclusive basis; the *contingency search firm*, an entity that attempts to place individuals in jobs with various companies and works on a nonexclusive basis; and the *Internet search*, where companies post opportunities and candidates post resumes.

Let's explore each of the four types of recruiters and recruitment methods, how best to work with them, and their benefits or disadvantages. As you read the descriptions of each type, take a critical look at their level of expertise and capabilities. Envision what their background might be like: their years of experience, area of expertise or specialization, level of maturity, judgment abilities, trust, and so on. Then determine with whom you would feel most comfortable sharing confidential career information and personal desires as you navigate your next best career step. In whose hands would you feel most confident placing your future and that of your family? Whom would you choose? After all, as I stated in the previous chapter, there are more than eight thousand executive recruiters worldwide, and growing. The choice *is* yours to make. Although you might not have a choice if a company chooses to only use its own in-house recruiters, after reading this and subsequent chapters you will be better prepared for and educated in how best to manage your working relationship with each of these types of recruiters, and ensure your chances of securing your next best career step.

In-House Recruiters

In-house recruiters (also known as *corporate recruiters*) are company employees who are housed in the human resource department—the "personnel department" or "employment office," as it had been known in years past and from which today's more progressive human resource departments have evolved. Some in-house recruiters are likely to have a wide variety of human resource responsibilities in addition to being charged with recruiting new employees, so their focus is not always solely in the area of recruiting.

I launched my career in executive recruiting as an in-house search professional with Hill and Knowlton, Inc., one of the world's largest and most-respected international public relations and public affairs firms. Although I began my tenure at Hill and Knowlton as a public relations professional in the consumer marketing division, management at the agency recognized my sharp ability to hire, nurture, and retain top talent. I was then given the opportunity to establish an in-house recruiting function in the domestic operations of the firm, which later expanded into the broader human resource area, and I thrived in the role. I considered this particular in-house recruitment role as an excellent opportunity to wed my years of public relations and operations experience with my ability to identify superior talent.

Prior to beginning my career as a search professional for the agency, I had gained many years of experience in hiring as a senior-level executive in the corporate communications function. During those years, I hired, fired, built, and disassembled departments; retained outside consultants; and counseled senior management, gaining significant hands-on experience in the recruiting process. Unfortunately for the reputation of the search profession and due to the lack of experience across most corporate functions on the part of recruiters, not everyone who serves in an in-house recruiting capacity has the ability to thoroughly qualify professionals' technical skills or their intuitive ability to be successful in the job.

With that as my preface, let me share with you some insights into the mysterious world of in-house recruiting and take a look at two polar opposite scenarios: the recruiter in a small company of perhaps 100 or fewer employees and the recruiter in a large company of nearly two hundred thousand employees.

Typically, in the smaller companies, broader human resource responsibilities also come under the purview of the recruiter—he will "wear a lot of hats," if you will. In a small company, the employee responsible for recruiting may also have duties that encompass managing compensation and benefits, payroll processing, performance evaluations, termination, and possibly serving as the receptionist. In terms of serving as a professional and proactive recruiter, this individual may be capable only of writing and posting advertisements in the "help wanted" section of the newspaper and culling through resumes of candidates who respond to the ads. He cannot possibly have the time, or the expertise, to properly assess your skills. Such employees have so many demands placed on them, that they usually do not have the time or training necessary to be topnotch recruitment specialists. That's just the way it is for a small company whose staffing needs are not as demanding as in larger organizations. They cannot afford, and neither do they necessarily need, the services of a professional recruiter.

Although this scenario may seem obvious to some, others who might blindly send a resume to a company do not realize who is reviewing their paperwork and conducting the resulting interview and evaluation process. Unfortunately for the company, the lack of professional recruiting skills on the part of the human resource employee may work in favor of the unqualified candidate, as the recruiter may not have the ability or time to assess the qualifications of the job seeker.

In desperation, particularly when facing a dearth of qualified candidates due to a tight labor market, the recruiter may hire a candidate on the spot. This hiring situation might result in the termination of the employee in a short period of time, which is costly to the company from the standpoint of lost productivity and a drop in morale. The in-house recruiter, however, might not recognize that the failure of the employee to perform was partially his own fault for not taking the time to fully qualify the candidate.

This small company, in-house recruiter example may appear to be somewhat extreme; however, it is not all that uncommon—especially if the recruiter's company is located in a small community where it is difficult to attract talent at any level of experience or expertise.

At the other end of the in-house recruiter spectrum is the professional recruiter employed by a very large organization. This professional typically has years of experience either in human resources or recruiting for a specific industry or function. Her experience will likely have been at a company that is focused on one industry, such as a large technology company, or on a function, such as finance. Typically, this individual is responsible only for recruiting candidates for that one company, or if it is a conglomerate, for companies owned or controlled by that entity. Although some corporate recruiters may be focused on one experience level, others hire at all levels. Again, this is usually determined by the size of the company.

Let's take a look at an example of how this type of recruiter operates, the department she works in, and the recruitment needs of the company for which she might work. Suppose the company is a $10 billion apparel retailer with more than one hundred eighty thousand employees worldwide—similar to the profile of a client for whom I recently conducted a retained search. A recruiter for this type of company is housed in the human resource department at the corporate level. In addition to the recruiting function, the human resource department houses other smaller, related departments within it, such as training, organizational effectiveness, compensation and benefits, workforce diversity, and also perhaps internal communications. For this size of operation and organization, the human resource department must be broad in scope and capabilities.

The recruiting department may be comprised of several employees, and its organizational chart might look like this, from top to bottom: a vice president of human resources, a director of recruitment, a few managers of recruitment, and possibly one or two associate and assistant managers of recruitment. It also may employ researchers and administrative assistants to support the recruitment staff. These individuals are specialists in their field, and their duties are focused exclusively on recruiting professionals at all levels throughout an organization. The department might be divided into recruiting specialties, according to function and/or title. For example, some recruiters might be assigned to conduct search for only the most senior-level management positions, such as director, vice president, or senior vice president. Some recruiters may be specialists in international recruiting for positions based in other countries. Others may be assigned to conduct search for departments housed only at the parent company, such as advertising, marketing, and merchandising, or for only the retail stores group. Still others may be focused only on filling hourly wage or nonexempt positions—typically those that involve work as sales associates in the retail stores.

Why would this company employ so many recruiters? One reason: A retail chain has a high composition of hourly or nonexempt employees, and the turnover rate in this category is high. For example, they might be hired at a retail store for a summer job, or as their first job out of high school, and possibly keep the job part time throughout college. Once they graduate, they will most likely enter their chosen career. Others might opt for a retail job following a divorce or retirement from another career. Still others might work retail jobs only seasonally. You can see how busy a recruiter in this industry for this size of company would be. Even though the retail recruiter might share some of the hiring responsibilities with district managers and store managers to keep the stores staffed properly during all seasons, recruiters must work diligently to find candidates, or *applicants,* at this level. Because of this heavy demand, in-house recruiters' time is stretched extremely thin. In fact, I've known of in-house recruiters who might be working on *40 assignments* at any given time. This clearly dilutes their ability to be effective and anything more than reactive to their company's needs.

Another reason a large retail company might employ a high ratio of recruiters compared with other similar-sized companies is because of rapid expansion. The global retail chain I am profiling in this example had expanded over the years in many areas—the types of stores, as well as domestically and internationally. The recruiters are charged with hiring employees for stores to be opened in the future and replacements for employees departing from stores already in operation. Needless to say, these recruiters have their hands full!

An advantage to you, the candidate, in working with an in-house recruiter is that you can send your paperwork directly to the company for which you are interested in working and know that an employee of that company will receive and process it. By *process,* I mean an administrative assistant-level employee will most likely take your resume that you either sent by e-mail or snail mail and open it, sort it according to position, alphabetize it, and possibly put it through a scanning process to identify key words to further sort it. Out of the hundreds of resumes the assistant received that day, your resume eventually might be reviewed by the senior-level recruiter who is assigned to conduct a search for the position you are seeking. Or it might *not* be. Still, you can usually count on your resume making it directly into the hands of a company employee.

Disadvantages to working directly with a prospective employer's human resource professionals, as opposed to being presented by an outside recruiter, are plentiful. One disadvantage is that all the potential employer can possibly learn about you when he receives your resume is what he discerns from glancing at *one document*. Rarely does the in-house recruiter have time to evaluate you beyond that resume—an excellent reason to write a crisp, compelling one. By contrast, when working with a professional executive recruiter, you have a third party presenting you in 3-D, as it were, because the recruiter will present to the prospective hiring executive multiple facets of your experience, skills, and personal attributes because we would have conducted an in-person interview and thoroughly assessed your qualifications. A one- or two-page resume cannot effectively serve its purpose, which is to present you in a compelling manner to a prospective employer.

Another disadvantage to sending your resume directly to a potential employer is confidentiality. One never knows who might see the paperwork you send—for that reason alone you need to decide how important confidentiality is to your job search. (This is especially true on the Internet, and I'll address this latter issue in the chapter.)

One more disadvantage to you directly sending your materials to a company has to do with responding to a blind ad—one of the riskiest methods of navigating your next career step. A *blind ad* is one that does not identify the name or address of the company, just the position it is seeking to fill. A company might run a blind ad because that firm does not want to divulge that it is losing its head of marketing, or is terminating that person, and wants to conduct a confidential search. The in-house recruiter might run an ad that reads, "Multibillion-dollar, Silicon Valley–based high-technology company is seeking a vice president of marketing to oversee a world-class department. . . . Attractive compensation package and benefits. Send your resume to Marketing Position, P.O. Box ABC, San Jose, California." Now, you might be a director-level executive who feels he is ready to take the next step to vice president, and you send your resume to the P.O. box. Next thing you know, your own company's human resource executive is calling you to advise you that she received your resume for the VP job at what you thought was at another company . . . not a very smart move strategically.

Related to this issue, it's prudent to use caution when seeking a job directly with a company. Do your research. Talk to people to learn as much as possible about the position, why it is open, and if they know anyone in the company, including in the human resource department. This will help you learn if you really want to seek a position in that company, and if you do, it will better equip you in preparing the materials you send to the organization. And if it's a blind ad, before responding to it, speak with as many of your contacts and mentors as possible to determine the company that is seeking to fill the position and why the spot is vacant. You want to do as much preparatory work as you can to bolster your chances of success while pursuing a new opportunity, particularly when working directly with a company's recruitment or staffing professionals.

Typically, at the more senior-executive level of search, it is not likely that the company will post an ad for a position but will instead work with an outside recruiter to identify candidates. At this executive level, it is difficult to merely post an advertisement in a newspaper and expect to attract the right candidate. And it is difficult for an in-house recruiter to directly contact a professional at a competitor company to try to recruit him or her, particularly when the corporate recruiter must get through layers of administrative assistants to do so. This is when a third-party executive search professional can be much more effective in identifying and recruiting candidates.

Retained or Contingency, That Is the Question!

Let's now examine the two types of third-party recruitment professionals—retained and contingency—why companies choose to work with them and why you would or would not wish to work with them from a candidate's perspective.

Retained Search

The most widely respected and preferred type of search is retained search. What is a retained search professional or firm, and why is it the preferred search method? In a retained search, a company signs a contract with an executive search firm and retains its services to fill a position or positions for an established fee that is paid by the company. The search firm is then entitled to an exclusive arrangement to fill the position. In exchange for this retained agreement, the search firm also provides management consulting services from the time the search is launched through its successful conclusion. Most retainer firms do not advertise their assignments—instead, they rely on a network of executive-level contacts they have developed and nurtured over the years as sources of candidates.

The executive search firm I founded in the mid-1980s, and for which I serve as president and CEO, is a retained firm. From this insider's perspective, let me share some of the best-kept secrets of the retained search process. With these insights you will gain a better understanding of how we operate and how best to work with us as you seek your next best career step. This knowledge will enable you to better discern the differences among the myriad types of recruiters when choosing whether to work with an executive recruiter who may mysteriously enter your life.

Although companies—and candidates—choose to work with a retained recruiting firm for many reasons, the foremost are for their contacts, counsel, and superior judgment about professionals. A retained recruiter maintains a database of thousands of professional contacts in a specific industry or function, or both, depending upon the size and scope of a firm. These contacts are typically at the mid- and senior-executive level—the level at which most companies use the services of outside search firms. These individuals are usually college educated and have a solid track record of success in a given profession. It also means they are leaders in an industry or discipline or both. In today's market, these professionals also command a compensation package comprised of a minimum

28

of a $100,000 base salary as well as a bonus eligibility defined as a percentage of the salary—usually 20 percent and higher, plus stock options, if employed by a publicly traded company; a health care benefits package; and often other perquisites, or "perks," such as cars, cell phones, computers, and so on.

In addition to the range of contacts and the credible relationships retained recruiters have with numerous professionals, a company retains the services of a professional executive recruiter for the strategic counsel the headhunter provides. This individual is not an order taker hired by a company to do this or do that. The recruiter provides strategic, fact-based counsel to the hiring executive throughout the entire search process. This involves several key steps as the search progresses, from the moment we first speak with the client in securing the assignment to the final placement of the professional—and continues even after the candidate has joined the client company. This counsel is given both to the client company as well as the candidate with whom we are discussing the career opportunity.

Now here's an inside peek at the process we employ at the search firm I lead. I want to share this multistep process with you so you will have a detailed and thorough understanding of how the process unfolds and know what to expect as a candidate or as a potential client. And you can gauge for yourself the level of energy and effort that a retained recruiter expends during a search—and the level of expertise needed to manage such an endeavor.

Step I: The Process

When our firm first approaches a company as a potential client, we start by providing the hiring executive with an overview of our capabilities as a search firm and a discussion of the mechanics of the search process. We impress upon them that our primary goal as an executive search and management consulting firm is to create success stories for our clients, their organizations, and the candidates whom we place.

We ensure that our clients understand that our success is also defined by the strategic management counsel we provide them throughout the entire search process, all in an effort to create the most successful match possible between the client organization and the successful candidate. Also key to the success of the client-recruiter and candidate-recruiter relationships is communication. We believe in apprising our clients of the status of their search assignments and our efforts on a regular basis. Client feedback and partnering with the executive recruiter as we travel down the road of executive search together is of great importance to the outcome of the process—a successful conclusion is the end goal for everyone involved. Similarly, we continually communicate with our candidates about their status in the search—even if it's a touch-base call every couple of weeks.

Step II: Due Diligence Immersion

Once we retain a client, we first conduct a thorough client briefing, or *due diligence session,* during which time the recruiter will meet with the company's executives to define the recruitment assignment and gain a better understanding of the corporate culture of the organization. We then combine the information we gleaned from these meetings with our own research and prepare an extensive job description for our firm's use throughout the search process and as a means to benchmark with our clients two factors: content of the job/what they ask us to pursue in the marketplace and the technical credentials and intangible qualities of talent we present. We send this position description to key sources who may be able to help us identify exceptional professionals who may become candidates, as well as to candidates we are targeting.

Step III: Research

Based on an understanding of the job specifications, our next phase of the search assignment is to conduct research. The objective of the research phase is not only to try to identify potential candidates for the position but, more broadly, to target companies where the ideal candidate may be located. In addition, during this phase we will contact key sources whose judgment we trust and whom we feel will be able to assist us in identifying the highest-quality professionals who may be viable candidates for this position. And, throughout this phase we are constantly evaluating and reevaluating what the market has to bear in terms of talent and how the marketplace is reacting to the opportunity, all in an effort to reach the end goal—successful placement of a candidate and conclusion of the search.

Step IV: Phone versus In-Person Interviews: When Do You Have Them and What Do You Do with Them?

Once we identify a list of individuals to contact, we will personally interview by telephone all those individuals who appear to be potential candidates for the position. This is a fairly exhaustive step, the objective of which will be to identify six to eight individuals who have the qualifications and background to hold the position and who indicate that they have a preliminary interest in exploring the opportunity. During this time, we will also be conducting thorough in-person interviews with the most highly qualified candidates to more precisely determine their viability to fill the position.

Throughout the interview period we communicate with our clients on a regular basis to review the candidates and their respective backgrounds to discuss their strengths and weaknesses and how they would fit into the organization.

During this process we provide our clients with biweekly written status reports until the search is completed.

Step V: Insights about Candidates

For each candidate we decide to present as part of our semifinalist panel of candidates, we will write a full narrative background including where they have worked, why they left various positions, responsibilities held in those positions, and so on. Most importantly, we include specific commentary about our perception of the individual's capability to meet/exceed our client's requirements—in essence, our definitive judgment about why the professional deserves to be considered. We expect to present four to six—and sometimes eight—semifinalist candidates for our client to consider. At this point, we will again answer any questions our clients have about the candidates, reach an agreement on those initial candidates that the client would like to interview in person, and then begin making those arrangements. We will also arrange whatever additional visits the client needs to allow the hiring entity the time needed to evaluate candidates, and enable candidates the opportunity to fully understand the position and scope of challenges.

Step VI: Stealth Referencing

After the client interviews and selects the top candidate from our panel and this professional expresses the same mutual interest and enthusiasm, we enter the stealth phase of referencing. By this time we will already have made two or three key preliminary reference checks, and we now pursue broader and deeper referencing while we begin to work with our client to design a compensation package that will ultimately be offered to the candidate.

A bit of insider's information for you: The way we ensure your confidentiality during the search process is to wait until the time of the offer to conduct in-depth reference checking because in almost all cases our candidates will be gainfully employed and we do not want to jeopardize their current employment. In addition, our clients may have specific questions regarding various areas of the candidate's background that they would like us to probe more thoroughly.

Step VII: The Negotiation Dance

Once the reference checks have been completed and the client is prepared to make the offer, we provide counsel as to the parameters of the compensation package and help in the negotiations between the client and candidate. We want to do whatever is necessary to help attract top talent to the client organization and ensure a smooth transition from the candidate's previous employment. By the way, negotiating compensation is oftentimes the most difficult and awkward part of the search process for both the hiring executive and the candidate. Hence, I've dedicated an entire section (Chapter 10) to discuss the art of finessing an offer.

Step VIII: Thanking Our Partners

Upon successful conclusion of the search assignment, we close the loop and contact all individuals with whom the search was discussed. We will inform them of the outcome and the name of the successful candidate, and we will thank them on behalf the client company for their interest in the opportunity or for their willingness to be helpful in recommending candidates.

Typically, to conduct a thorough search assignment and identify the most highly qualified professionals, it takes approximately ninety days, depending on what the market has to bear as well as the timing involved with scheduling interviews between the hiring executive and the candidates, from the start of the search to the first day of employment of the successful candidate.

Contingency Search—The Other Half?

Contingency search firms' roots are somewhat similar to those of retained firms, but unlike their "cousins" that conduct search at the professional or executive level, contingency firms target the nonprofessional work force. About half the search firms in existence today operate on a contingency basis, while the other half practice on a retained basis.

Contingency firms essentially evolved from the employment agencies of the early 1950s that worked with post–World War II boom companies overloaded with a demand for employees. To attract applicants for positions they were seeking to fill on behalf of these companies, employment agencies would run ads in newspapers; if they did not have a specific position to fill, they would post an ad inviting applicants to register with them for future jobs. For this service, the applicant might have paid a fee to be included on their roster of applicants awaiting a call for their dream job. The fee might have been a small percentage of the candidate's anticipated annual compensation. As time passed and competition for this level of employee intensified, the employer would pay the fee, and the contingency firm would advertise "Fee Paid by Employer" prominently in its job listings.

Over time as terminology changed, these agencies evolved into adopting the language of their retained firm cousins and dropped the word *agency* from their nomenclature in an effort to achieve a more professional image and status. However, let me tell you a secret: To truly match the level of expertise of and be considered on par with a retained firm, a contingency firm needs to do much more than just change its terminology. Until these firms change their methods, approach, level

34

of assignments, and other fundamental ways of operation, the contingency moniker will forever be attached.

Allow me to give you an overview of the methods that contingency search firms employ in seeking candidates. You should decide if this is the type of organization that you would prefer to have help you navigate your career—or, if you are a company, if your recruitment needs can be met with this approach.

The foremost method that today's contingency firms use to attract potential candidates remains pretty much the same as that of the traditional employment agency: They run numerous advertisements in high-circulation newspapers, trade publications, and now perhaps on the Internet. This is the fastest way to reach a broad number of applicants or candidates for the positions they are seeking to fill—typically below the managerial level and with compensation far below a base salary of $100,000.

Then you, the candidate, respond to these ads and send a resume to the contingency firm. What happens next? Well, let's take a look at one scenario. Your resume might be stamped "received and dated" and then placed in the search firm's database and/or files. Then a recruiter might perform a perfunctory comparison between your resume and opportunities known to him. This recruiter might call you and tell you he is conducting a search for an exciting position at such and such a company, and would you be interested? You might be delighted at the prospect of having your resume forwarded to this outstanding company and express a strong interest in the opportunity. The recruiter will then send your resume to the company, along with dozens of others, and like the old adage of throwing a handful of spaghetti against the wall, the contingency recruiter hopes (and prays, frankly) that one sticks! Not a highly effective approach.

Now, why would the recruiter do this? First, it is critical for you to recognize that as a contingency firm, a company has *not* retained the firm to conduct a search on its behalf. It does not have an "exclusive" on the search, unlike retained firms. The firm primarily serves as a forwarding mechanism and a conduit (albeit a long-shot conduit) to a possible job. Second, because the contingency firm gets paid only when a placement is made, its recruiters can't invest a lot of time interviewing, qualifying, and getting to know candidates. The more candidates the firm "processes" and sends to the client, the better the contingency recruiter increases his odds of placing someone and reaching his end goal of the pot of gold at the end of the rainbow.

The other true danger associated with contingency search is that the recruiter might also send your resume *without* your permission to companies. But that oftentimes doesn't really matter to the contingency recruiter—volume counts. Remember: The more resumes they send, the likelier they'll get to the pot of gold. Never mind that you don't know about it or that your qualifications aren't quite right for the position. So off your resume goes to a number of companies that may very well be undesirable to you.

Unlike the retained recruiter, the contingency recruiter is willing to shove a square peg in a round hole. She will get paid for the placement, and it is the employer's problem if the fit isn't right. And, although the client might feel a bit burned by the experience, she can't be too harsh on the recruiter because the client knew the rules of the game when he entered into the contingency agreement. The firm or individual practitioner provides a certain level of service and no more. This is why contingency firms have earned a reputation as what many professionals in the marketplace describe as "body brokers."

Contingency recruiters have become experts in the business of arm twisting to get you to accept a position that you do not feel is in your best interest. Retained recruiters do not, or *should* not, utilize such coercive tactics. In fact, as I stated in section on the retained search, it is definitely *not* in the retained headhunter's best interest to place you in a position that is not your next best career step and that does not make you a satisfied candidate because he will need to relaunch the search should you choose to leave the position. It makes no sense for anyone to use such strong-arm tactics, not even for the contingency recruiter, in my opinion.

One final note: Certain companies that have many positions to fill will work with many contingency recruiters, as doing so can increase the odds of filling the positions. After all, clients may assume that multiple firms working on their behalf, rather than only one, will serve them better. Why not have several contingency recruiters working on the same assignment? It only costs the client one fee for each position filled—at least until that horrifying moment when multiple firms present the same candidate! This is where everyone involved enters treacherous waters. It is therefore in the best interest of the contingency firm to fill the easiest assignments first, and because there is no obligation to present any candidates for the more difficult, time-consuming searches, it may beat its competitors at their own game. But where does that leave the client? Probably in the crossfire. Even more important, where does that leave the innocent, unsuspecting candidate? Caught in a *huge* career mess.

One situation I recall from my tenure at Hill and Knowlton was the day one of our senior executives asked me to interview a professional whom he had met through a colleague and whom he wanted to hire. At the conclusion of my interview, the woman expressed her confusion about the fact that a contingency recruiter told her that she could not accept the position unless Hill and Knowlton paid the firm a fee. Not only did we not have a contract with the search firm, but since when does a search firm "own" talent! I advised her not to worry about the situation, and I proceeded to set the record straight with the contingency firm. After lengthy arguments, I finally had to resort to having our parent company's lawyers explain the fallacies in the search firm's position to the recruiter. It was simple: The firm had no contract with us, it had not even obtained permission from the candidate to "represent" her, and therefore, we were not obligated to pay any fee. What a messy situation for the candidate to have to be involved in as she navigated her career—a situation into which she was forced as a result of a contingency firm's greed.

Throughout my years in executive search, I've heard both good and bad stories about contingency recruiters. There are some out there who are highly reputable and serve a niche that is beneficial to corporate America. However, *candidate beware*! Take heed at my word to be cautious in working with contingency recruiters. And after reviewing the methods of both types of practitioners, who would you want helping you to manage your career—the retained search professional or the contingency recruiter?

The Dollars and Cents of It

The leading retained search firms charge fees based on a pre-determined percentage of the estimated first-year's cash compensation of the candidate. This includes the base salary target, annual cash bonus, and sign-on bonuses, if any; sometimes firms will even invoice against the market value of the stock options. The firm is compensated regardless of whether a candidate is placed in the position, as the firm is paid for its management consulting services and its overall efforts, not just for sending a handful of resumes to the client, which is what contingency firms typically do. This percentage typically ranges from 30 to 33.3 percent of this package. Most of these firms invoice monthly during the three- to four-month search process. And some firms also charge an additional 15 to 20 percent, off the top, to cover out-of-pocket expenses to avoid having to itemize their expenditures.

For multiple, similar searches for the same company, retained firms sometimes will consider working on a sliding scale—that is, 30 percent for the first search, 27.5 percent for the second, 25 percent for the third, and so on. Or they might assess a flat 25 percent for all three or four searches of the same type.

If unforeseen circumstances necessitate the cancellation of a retained search within the three-month period over which a retainer is billed, our firm will charge only for the pro rata portion of the retainer to that particular date. If, on the other hand, the search continues beyond a three-month period, we will continue working on the project, charging only for out-of-pocket expenses.

So if a retained firm gets paid regardless of whether it finds a candidate for the search it is assigned to complete, you are probably asking yourself, what is the incentive to find candidates? First, a firm would not be in business long if it merely accepted assignments and never completed a search. In the history of my firm, nearly all of the searches we have accepted have been successfully completed. Those not completed usually were due to reasons on the client company side, such as a reorganization causing the position to be eliminated, or perhaps after months of seeking candidates outside the company, management decides to promote an employee to the post from within the company. There are myriad reasons why retained firms work hard to complete their assignments. Clearly it is in the best interest of the search firm to identify a candidate for the opportunity for all concerned, particularly for the reputation and viability of the retained search firm!

And now, what is the fee structure of contingency firms? Fundamentally, a contingency firm receives payment for its efforts only *if and when* a candidate it presents for the position is actually hired by the client company—payment is contingent upon placing a candidate. That's where the *contingency* terminology comes in. What contingency firms charge may vary widely, from the 30 to 33.3 percent of the retained firms to a fee schedule of 1 percent per $1,000 up to a maximum of 35 percent of the candidate's first-year compensation. Contingency firms might also ask for a fee from candidates for various services performed, including writing resumes, consultation, and eventual placement. The rules change according to the type of candidate and position the recruiter is seeking to fill. And sometimes it's based on what they can convince a client to pay.

Given that retained firms receive fees regardless of whether a candidate is placed, why wouldn't every firm be retained in nature rather than contingency? It may be the case that every firm would *like* to conduct retained searches, but not every firm or individual headhunter is *qualified* to do so. A retained search professional is what every head-hunter aspires to be—or *should* aspire to be. And the more time you spend navigating your career, the more you will experience the difference in professionalism and expertise when working with retained search executives compared with those who are *not* with retained firms. You will also see that headhunters who are not retained might intimate that they *are* in an attempt to gain instant credibility and respect from both prospective clients and candidates. Again, *candidate beware!*

Internet Search—The Newest Methodology of Career Navigation?

Without question, the Internet spawned a whole new avenue of career navigation and executive search methodology—both for the candidate and hiring entity's perspective. However, at this stage in the infancy of Internet recruiting, it is definitely not a panacea for the issues that we in the executive search field have to manage and that you, the candidate, confront in navigating your career. And in my opinion, it never will be. It *never* will replace traditional recruiting methods in totality, and neither will it be able to make the ultimate judgment call that recruiters are expected to make—that of whether a professional can be successful in a specific position. It does not and cannot serve the complex needs of the candidate or the client company in totality.

Internet recruiting is very similar to classified advertising in high-circulation newspapers—posting ads on the Internet has the potential to reach an extraordinary number of individuals. And in the event you did not know, online postings were spawned from classified ads posted on newspapers' Web sites! However, there are some advantages to recruiting online, but it depends upon whether you are the hiring executive or the candidate as well as on the intended goal. Rule number one dictates that you reach your target audience. Do Internet searches reach their intended audience? And, do you, the candidate, find the Internet to be the source of the type or level of positions you are seeking as you navigate your career? And, like classified ads in publications, the job postings on the Internet only reach individuals who are actively looking for jobs. In fact, according to a 1999 research report compiled by interbiznet.com, a niche consulting firm, the composition of those who are Web users and do or do not visit Internet recruiting sites is as follows: 5 percent are unemployed and visit recruiting sites; 10 percent are employed, are active in looking for a new job, and visit recruiting sites; and 15 percent are employed, are thinking about seeking a new job, and visit recruiting sites. The remaining 71 percent are employed and *do not* visit the job boards. *Seventy-one percent!* And those employed individuals are the candidates that companies primarily seek because they are gainfully employed and theoretically successful at what they do. The questions you need to ask yourself are whether you would feel comfortable using this medium and whether this is an appropriate or potential career navigation avenue.

Clearly, these postings cannot replace the efforts by a headhunter who actually *hunts* for qualified candidates through direct contact, usually by calling an individual either as a targeted candidate or a source of candidates and conducting both telephone and in-person interviews. This human-touch element *cannot* be replaced by online recruiting. Nothing that I've seen that's available today on the Internet can replicate this critical aspect of executive search—not ads, not online assessments, and not streaming-video interviewing. One cannot expect online recruiting techniques to be up to par with executive search firms that have been perfecting their professional methodologies for more than six decades. After all, it's difficult to imagine that the World Wide

Web, created *only* in 1991, could already surpass what the executive search industry has mastered.

The roots of the Internet can be traced to the 1950s with the advent of communications satellites launched in space. At this time and during the next few decades, it was only defense personnel and academics who were able to use computer network communications. General consumer use of what evolved to be the World Wide Web was not broadly established until the late 1980s, when personal computers were first sold with free software from America Online (AOL), CompuServe, and Prodigy to enable the now traditional dial-up access to the Internet.

Online recruiting can be traced to that same point in time when newspaper and journal publishers began replicating their classified advertising sections online, companies with web sites started posting opportunities, job boards were created, and dot-com companies began so-called e-cruiting sites. Today, there are more than two hundred thousand Web sites actively engaged in recruiting candidates according to the interbiznet.com report referenced earlier. These e-cruiting sites are comprised of the following varied recruitment sources and methods: "pure play" job boards; those that list jobs and provide other online career services, such as hotjobs.com, careerbuilder.com, headhunter.net, and job-shop.net (to name a few); traditional Web portals that provide links to job sites and have strategic alliances with other job boards, such as Yahoo!, AOL, and AltaVista; online recruiters such as careercentral.com, Korn/Ferry's FutureStep.com, and Heidrick & Struggles' Leadersonline .com; newspaper publishers, such as individual publications' classified postings to a consortium of 80 newspapers that created careerpath.com; recruitment advertising companies, including TMP Worldwide and its monster.com and Topjobs's topjobs.net; online career fairs, such as westech.com and 1-jobs.com; and, the Web sites of numerous corporations, staffing companies, and other sources that are created and updated daily.

How do they work? Let's take a quick look at what some of the leading sites are touting as to how they serve both candidates and employers, and while you review this section, give some thought to how you would feel about online recruiting as the only option to navigating your career.

Company: TMP Worldwide.

Site: monster.com.

Ranking: #1.

Founded: 1994.

Services to Candidates: More than four hundred fifty thousand job postings in the United States. Candidates can create up to five online resumes and cover letters to use to apply online to jobs; activate your resume so that employers can view it or store it privately for your own use; track your online job applications; create automatic Job Search Agents that e-mail you when a job listing matches your criteria; and get news and articles tailored to your interests. Also links to ResumeZapper, a service to e-mail a resume to thousands of recruiters.

Fees to Candidates: None for basic service; links to other services through other sites entail additional costs: For example, ResumeZapper is $49.99 per use.

Services to Employers: Access to more than nine million job seekers; resume search agents to automatically search for resumes by functionality; resume prescreening technology; jobs posted for up to 60 days.

Fees to Employers: $275 for a single, 60-day U.S. job posting (nonrefundable); volume discounts apply; annual subscription rates to access the resume database begin at $5,500 for one user.

Additional Services: Monster.com also offers "ChiefMonster" for executive-level positions and "MonsterTalent Market" for freelance and temporary contract talent. TMP Worldwide is also the parent of LAI Worldwide and TASA Worldwide traditional executive search firms and is the number one Yellow Pages ad company.

Company: Headhunter.net.

Site: Headhunter.net (merged with CareerMosaic, formerly ranked #2, in July 2000).

Ranking: #2.

Founded: 1996.

Services to Candidates: More than two hundred fifty thousand job postings with more than ten thousand companies in the United States; career assessment; resume services and distribution; library/company research; compensation calculators; relocation information; newsletter; reference checking information; interview tips; and links to training information, executive recruiters, and career expos.

Fees to Candidates: None for basic service; candidates wishing upgrade options for maximum visibility and access to educational resources are assessed fees; links to other services through other sites entail additional costs: For example, ResumeZapper is $49.99 per use.

Services to Employers: Access to more than six million job seekers; search more than eight hundred thousand resumes. It offers tailored employer services for cost-effective convenience, including a credit card–based "EaseEPost" option for companies posting fewer than ten jobs per month and "Performance Posting" options to maximize reach as well as links to individualized "Company Profile" Web sites, allowing recruiters and employers to post detailed job listings directly online. Cross-posted on more than three hundred forty job boards.

Fees to Employers: Range from a $50 economy fee for entry-level and administrative candidates in noncompetitive markets; a $75 basic fee for general positions in mid- and noncompetitive markets; a $100 standard fee for key management positions such as sales, marketing, accounting, finance, and engineering in midlevel and competitive markets; and a $125 priority fee for hard-to-fill positions in the nation's most competitive markets. Positions are posted up to 90 days.

Additional Services: Distinguishes itself from other sites by providing job seekers with complete privacy when searching and applying for jobs. For employers, it offers a "VIP Resume Search"—a members-only option giving employers access to more than five hundred fifty thousand hireable professionals for the "freshest resumes" by date posted, job category, location, and experience.

Company: Korn/Ferry International—Futurestep.com.
Site: Futurestep.com.
Ranking: Highest-visibility executive search site for management professionals ($75,000–$150,000 base salary).
Founded: 1998.
Services to Candidates: Post professional information on a personalized Web page that only Futurestep recruiters can access. Once posted, candidates will be considered for opportunities with Futurestep clients worldwide. Receive customized salary feedback; use customized assessment tools to help you manage your career, as well as decision-making and communications styles; access other career management content and tools; and receive career management articles and newsletters via e-mail.
Fees to Candidates: None.
Services to Employers: Its site states that Futurestep gives its clients the reach and speed of the Internet combined with the professionalism and expertise of retained executive search, calling it "clicks and mortars." It states it offers the best of online recruiting technology, including video interviewing and a global candidate database fully assessed for cultural fit with the client organization.
Fees to Employers: Same as a traditional retained search fee—30 percent of the candidate's first-year cash compensation.
Additional Services: The site states: "Plus the best of the world's leading executive search firm (Korn/Ferry International) with over 30 years of understanding the recruiting marketplace and helping world-class organizations build their management teams to achieve their strategic goals." However, Futurestep's operations and database are separate from Korn/Ferry's. Futurestep also is a partnership between Korn/Ferry and *The Wall Street Journal,*

in whose "Marketplace" section it also posts job advertisements.

These are just three examples of the thousands of recruitment sites on the Internet. An entire book could be written that evaluates and assesses their value to the candidate. In general, what results can a candidate expect from using online recruiting sites to navigate their career compared to the services traditional executive search firms provide? In my opinion, a moderate amount. There is just no comparison to what a candidate can gain in her job search from interfacing with a human recruiter compared with what an online service offers. As I stated in the beginning of this section, success through online recruiting can typically be found at the entry-level/lower-level positions and sometimes midmanagement positions with annual base salaries of up to $80,000. The Internet might be one of the best resources for individuals who are launching their careers or have a few years of experience. In fact, in a recent article in *The Wall Street Journal,* a reporter wrote about how hot recruiting can be on the Internet, particularly for technology professionals who are in the early years of their career. The article stated:

> Recruiters have honed their online techniques down to a science, and their methods work especially well at night, when traffic on the Web is low and the system moves data faster. Many stay up past 2 A.M. combing job sites, surfing chat rooms, digging out fresh resumes on personal Web pages, posting help-wanted ads and sending e-mails. Candidates with technical skills that are especially in demand often find themselves bombarded with calls and e-mails within minutes of posting a resume online. Recruiters say that the window for making overtures closes quickly. "I hate to think of the number of times I have heard, 'If you would have called 10 minutes ago. . . . I just accepted an offer,' " [said a recruiter of a potential candidate].

Conversely, I recently made a presentation on the topic of navigating one's career to a group of 300 professionals who were attending an international conference of investor relations practitioners, and I included a discussion on Internet recruiting as part of this presentation. During the question-and-answer period I asked how many in the audience had been hired into a company from an Internet posting. Of the 300, 2 raised their hands. I asked both of them what position they were hired for, and both responded that they had been entry-level roles.

In my view, the Internet can certainly be of tremendous benefit in one's career navigation and to recruiters as well— up to a point. For the candidate, it serves as an excellent resource for information on companies and links to other sites; posting resumes; and an improved, more contemporary version of newspaper-based classified ads. For the recruiter, it can serve as a great avenue for marketing a certain level of career opportunity, as a good tool for tracking resumes, and even as a way to identify key technical skills through special software programs. However, try as they might, those who program these sites cannot possibly replace the human contact needed to accurately assess cultural fit, character traits, or other qualities beyond the skill sets needed for many positions.

Now that you know all about the types of executive recruiters, let's examine the resources available to the job seeker to identify and target the search firm best suited to his or her career goals.

———

Secret: How do I love thee, let me count the ways . . . when they need you, they love you, when they don't, who are you? I believe relationships are a two-way street. Run the other direction when a headhunter wants only to broker your body.

CHAPTER 3

Taking the Mystery out of Finding an Executive Search Firm Most Suited to Your Career Goals

Unless a recruiter has contacted you at some point in your career, it may be a mystery to you as to how to make contacts in the executive search profession. What resources are available to you, the job seeker, and how do you identify and use them? Exactly how do you find the right executive search firm to help move your career forward? Do you start by scanning the Internet for search firms' Web sites? Do you visit your local bookstore and grab an armload of career books from the business section? Do you ask a trusted colleague or mentor whom you should call? Or is it as simple as scanning your local telephone book? Where *do* you begin? Therein lies the mystery! The task certainly seems daunting, with more than eight thousand executive search professionals and eighteen hundred search firms worldwide as potential targets. Where do you turn for the best information to help shape your decision-making process?

Although there is no one simple answer to these questions, in this chapter I'll unravel the mystery of identifying an executive search firm most suited to your career goals. Let's examine how best to identify and maximize your recruitment resources.

Recruitment Resources in the Marketplace

Fundamentally, there are two types of resources upon which you may draw to identify the executive search firm and the type of recruiter most suited to your career needs: the network of professionals in your life who are your trusted confidants and can introduce you to other contacts who may know recruiters to recommend to you and the research you conduct through directories of recruiters, Web sites of recruitment firms and corporations, and print publications, including newspapers, industry newsletters, business magazines, association journals, and career books. It is important that you fully leverage and utilize both types of resources as you conduct your job search and continue to shape your career. Let's examine some of your options.

Leveraging Your Professional and Personal Network

As you mark a certain point in your life and career, you will undoubtedly have developed a trustworthy network of professional and personal contacts. This group is likely to have served as an important support network for you on myriad levels. For example, your first important relationships in your life, developed during your school years, will have been forged with key family members, friends, teachers, and counselors. These trusted relatives, peers, and educators may have supported you through some tough situations during those growth years, including providing guidance in deciding which college to attend and assisting you through the application process and during your course work. Similarly, at another stage in your life, you might tap members of this same group for their counsel in recommending a real estate broker, a physician, an attorney, or other professionals. You have trusted these key contacts to help you shape some of the most important decisions you make throughout your lifetime. These personal contacts become your lifelong mentors.

Identifying individuals you can trust in your personal life may have been a simple process for you. However, you may be among the many who might be unsure how to secure a group of trustworthy professional contacts to guide them through their *career-related* choices. Leveraging relationships with these mentors to identify the executive search firm and recruiter most suited to your needs will be a springboard to your success, and I'll discuss this in greater detail in Chapter 12. For now, let me give you a brief synopsis of how best to identify them and glean their knowledge for career purposes.

Mentors, Colleagues, and Peers

Similar to the mentoring relationships you have developed in your personal life, you are likely to have interfaced with various individuals in your professional life—colleagues and peers—with whom you have developed a rapport and whom you have grown to trust. You feel you can confide in these coworkers on just about any topic. You share with some of these colleagues your aspirations, successes, and shortcomings—both personal and professional. You know you can rely on these individuals to serve as a sounding board for you, to give you solid advice and counsel both during crises and in day-to-day life. Some of these individuals may be prior immediate supervisors whom you respect and to whom you have always turned for guidance. Others may be coworkers from other departments or within your group with whom you have developed a solid give-and-take relationship. These contacts comprise some of your *professional mentors*.

Your camaraderie with and trust in your mentors will become invaluable to your professional growth. Although some of you may have reached the point in your career where you already have tapped into this resource on numerous occasions, you may not have thought to ask this group whom they might recommend you contact in the executive search profession to further your career. This trusted resource is the best place to start seeking counsel about finding and working with a recruiter best suited to your needs. They probably have been down the path; they know the drill, and they know you. They are by far the ideal resource to tap for guidance.

However, you should use caution in determining who is a true mentor, as the key word in your mentoring relationships is *trust!* You want to be certain that by asking a colleague how you can identify highly professional headhunters with whom you can develop a relationship, he or she is not going to run to your boss and disclose the fact that you might be seeking a new job. Trust is a critical factor in soliciting guidance in this area.

Professional and Industry Trade Organizations

If you are not a member of a professional or industry trade organization, you should identify the associations that most closely relate to your career path and become a member of one or two immediately. This can be a tremendously valuable resource for a variety of career needs, not to mention identifying contacts that can recommend executive search firms and headhunters. The organizations or associations that will best serve your career needs will be those that relate to your functional expertise or industry of choice. For example, if you are a marketing and public relations professional working in the health care industry, your choice of *functional* associations to join would include the American Marketing Association, the Public Relations Society of America, and the International Association of Business Communicators, whereas your *industry* association options might include the American Association of Health Plans, National Managed Health Care Congress, and the American College of Healthcare Executives, just to name a few. Networking with members of these organizations can be vital to your career growth.

By joining these associations and becoming an active member in their meetings, seminars, conferences, and other events, you will develop a tremendous group of professional contacts and increase your visibility among leaders in the function and industry in which you wish to succeed. Once you have established your contacts within these organizations, ask them if they have worked with an executive search firm or headhunter that they would recommend to you. Ideally, they will know the firms and professionals who best serve the function and the industry in which you work. (I'll discuss in greater detail how search firms specialize in function and industry later in this chapter.) They will also know the recruiters who do not necessarily have the highest professional standards and whom you want to avoid. What better choice than to seek advice from these veterans in the discipline and industry you are targeting? And they will likely share some war stories with you about their own experiences working with headhunters. This firsthand knowledge is key to increasing your knowledge about the executive search profession and those recruiters who may be handling searches for career opportunities attractive to you.

If you are unable to become active in a professional or trade association due to time constraints, at the very least become a member. Your membership will provide you with a directory of members and key contacts in the organization. You may then contact the president, membership director, or chapter head and ask them to recommend search firms and recruiters with whom their members have worked successfully. Most will be able to make such a recommendation.

Other Organizations

Although professional organizations will more than likely generate the best leads for your selection of executive search firms, you may wish to tap into other resources such as community and social organizations in which you are currently involved or plan to become involved. Don't overlook members of athletic clubs, youth groups, college alumni networks, fraternal and religious organizations, and charitable organizations. Many opinion leaders and civic-minded individuals are members of these groups and can provide you with a wealth of career advice and counsel about choosing an executive search firm. Although you should not bombard them with questions in the middle of a fundraising event or tennis match, get to know them and ask them to join you for lunch to discuss your career. Build and nurture a relationship with them and seek their guidance. You may be surprised at how willing and eager these community leaders will be to help you.

Executive Search Directories and Other Publications

Once you have maximized your professional and personal contacts and mentors as resources for finding headhunters, unequivocally the best resource for identifying executive search firms and individual recruiters, both retained and contingency, is through two directories—Hunt-Scanlon Publishing Company's *The Job Seekers Guide to Executive Recruiters* and Kennedy Information's *The Directory of Executive Recruiters*. These companies publish comprehensive directories, both for job seekers and for the hiring corporation, and both publish career guidance books and newsletters and also market extensive databases of information on companies and executives. Each firm also has its own Web site offering extensive services for candidates and hiring executives. Here's a brief overview of what's available from these publishers.

Hunt-Scanlon Corporation

According to its literature, Hunt-Scanlon Corporation provides "market intelligence, industry rankings, online research, database products, and advisory services on executive search and Internet recruiting." It offers "products and services relating to executive search, staffing, online recruiting, human resources and corporate diversity, for the candidate and the hiring entity."

The firm publishes several directories, career guidance books, newsletters, market intelligence studies, and Web sites that can prove invaluable to you as you navigate your career. The most useful of these resources for you, the candidate, is *The Job Seekers Guide to Executive Recruiters,* a more-than-five-hundred-page "pocket guide" that contains the names, addresses, and phone numbers as well as industry, function, and geographic and salary concentrations of more than fifty-five hundred executive recruiters across the United States. The firm also publishes more segmented directories: *The Job Seeker's Guide to Wall Street Recruiters* and *The Job Seeker's Guide to Silicon Valley Recruiters,* focusing on two of today's hottest employment sectors: financial services and information technology, respectively. In the next few pages I'll tell you more about how to best find the firm and recruiter by function, industry, and type, to help you navigate your career.

Hunt-Scanlon also publishes more extensive directories for human resource professionals and recruiters that the firm states are "a key source of vital information" for these professionals "who rely on the most comprehensive Who's Who in retained and contingency executive recruiting." The directories are "packed with information to help you evaluate more than 6,000 executive recruiters in more than 1,000 executive search firms." For those seeking executive search firms overseas, Hunt-Scanlon publishes *Executive Recruiters International: Europe, Asia/Pacific, Australia, South America and Africa,* providing comprehensive information on nearly one thousand executive recruiters and 580 international affiliate search firm offices located in more than thirty countries.

For the job seeker or recruiter seeking contacts in corporations, Hunt-Scanlon's four-volume *Select Guide* directory set offers corporate data, cross-indexing, and more than one hundred thousand executives in four major functions (human resources, finance, sales and marketing, and information technology) in more than ten thousand leading companies throughout the United States. These listings include a company profile, addresses, phone numbers, industry classifications, revenues, number of employees, public/private, parent companies, subsidiaries, and divisions.

The firm's two primary Web-based resources include *ExecutiveSelect,* an online database of executives in corporate America that a subscriber to the service can access at any time, with unlimited use. Similar to Hunt-Scanlon's *Select Guide,* its online *ExecutiveSelect* provides access to lists of more than one hundred thousand executives at 10,000 companies in the United States through its "Leaders on the Move" executive tracking service.

Its recruiterlink.com site enables a job seeker or hiring executive to identify executive search firms and individual recruiters in the United States, Canada, Mexico, South America, and other overseas regions through a sophisticated and user-friendly search engine. The site invites you to perform a query, and you simply click on that button. It then gives you instructions on how to perform your query, asking you to select the multiple criteria to narrow your search. For example, if you know the name of the executive search firm or recruiter you are seeking, you simply put that information into the specified boxes and the results will display name, address, phone number, and other pertinent information on the firm or individual.

If you are conducting a general query to find a recruiting firm or individual recruiter, you may input key information, and it will search by various criteria, including location (state, city, region, and country), industry practice of recruiter, functional practice of recruiter, average salary level handled, lowest salary level handled, and off-limits policy. Click on a button that states "Display companies based on your selections" and voilà: Depending upon how many categories you checked, from a handful to hundreds of executive search firms and recruiters will be displayed.

And through its Hunt-Scanlon Advisors, the firm provides comprehensive market intelligence studies, trend surveys, and forecast indicator reports, among other services. In addition, it operates The Institute for Corporate Diversity, a leading diversity database and research publisher whose products include *Diversity in Corporate America,* a 500-page reference directory featuring information on executives managing diversity programs in some of America's largest organizations. According to the firm, this resource enables you to locate peers, consultants, state and federal agencies, benchmarking, and associations. It also offers a similar service online through DiversityOnline.com—which it states is the largest Internet site dedicated to corporate diversity today and includes the most complete e-commerce market for diversity-related products.

The price of these directories and online services ranges from free for some of the research that is posted on the firm's Web site, such as a simple query to locate a search firm or recruiter, to $1,250 for an annual unlimited-use subscription to *ExecutiveSelect Online.* Hunt-Scanlon's most useful, and perhaps most popular, guide for the candidate, *The Job Seekers Guide to Executive Recruiters,* is $49.95. Although most of these guides are available only by directly contacting the publisher, through Hunt-Scanlon's Web site, or by subscription, *The Job Seekers Guide* can be purchased at most major bookstores.

Kennedy Information, LLC

Another leading resource for executive career management is Kennedy Information. According to its marketing literature, Kennedy Information offers information on select professional services, including management consulting, executive recruiting, and investor relations. In addition to publishing eight newsletters, three magazines, research reports, and a host of Web sites, the firm publishes several executive search firm and recruiter directories for both the job seeker and the hiring authority.

For the candidate, Kennedy's *The Directory of Executive Recruiters*, or as it has become known, the "Red Book," is a 1,320-page directory that lists more than twelve thousand executive recruiters at more than five thousand search firms in the United States, Canada, and Mexico. It provides an index of firms and recruiters by management functions, industries, geography, key principals, and 550 individual recruiter specialties. Updated annually, the listings include comprehensive contact data, including phone, fax, e-mail, and Web addresses.

Specialized directories that the firm publishes include the *International Directory of Executive Recruiters*, a comprehensive listing of thousands of recruiters in 1,600 firms located in more than sixty countries outside of North America; *The Directory of Legal Recruiters*, a directory that lists nearly eight hundred recruiters in 320 law firms and indexed by 33 legal specialties, 22 industry focus areas, and 109 individual recruiter specialties and geographic locations; and other directories, such as the *Directory of Outplacement and Career Management Firms*, *Directory of Executive Temporary Placement Firms*, and *Kennedy's Pocket Guide to Working with Executive Recruiters*.

Supplementing these directories is online information that replicates some of the publisher's directories. For example, Kennedy Information Online includes an executive recruiter database that enables the user to download full contact information for the executive recruiters in a specific industry, function, geography, salary range, and other query topics. Its more advanced ExecutiveAgent.com provides both a listing of recruiters and an interactive tool that enables the user to e-mail a resume directly to the headhunter she chooses. ExecutiveAgent.com guides the user through a six-step process that allows you to choose your preferred industries and function, create your cover letter and (you'll be asked if you are actively seeking or passively seeking a job, the salary range you'd prefer, and where you'd like to work), view listings of firms matching your requirements within your geographic preference, and then e-mail your resume to all of the firms you identified.

Costs for these directories and online services range from nothing for some of the research and information published on its Web site, as well as a portion of its ExecutiveAgent tool, to a few hundred dollars for its directories. To download information on the recruiters listed on the Web site's database, you will be charged $1 per contact for the first 100, with a $30 minimum order, and $.25 for each additional contact after 100. To take advantage of the resume–e-mailing service, you will be charged a one-time use fee of $99. Kennedy's *Directory of Executive Recruiters* (for the candidate) is $47.95. Similar to Hunt-Scanlon's information, directories and publications can be purchased directly from the publisher, by subscription, or through Kennedy's Web site, and its *Directory of Executive Recruiters* is available in most major bookstores and in many public libraries.

Global versus Boutique Firms

In using these publishers' directories and any other information you uncover through your research in identifying executive recruiting firms, it will help you to understand the differences between firms that are classified as *global* from those that are *boutique* and the difference between industry and functional specialization of these firms. By understanding how firms are classified and how they break out into areas of specialization, you will then be able to cull down the list of recruiters you plan to target in your career navigation process for optimal results.

Let's take a look at the difference between global and boutique search firms and how to target the firm that best suits your own particular needs. A global search firm is typically one that conducts executive searches worldwide, has multiple branch offices with numerous recruiters, and is a generalist firm—one that conducts searches in all industries and functional disciplines. It also is most likely to recruit only at the senior-management level. A boutique firm, on the other hand, is likely to have one or a few offices with fewer recruiters; it may recruit locally, nationally, and sometimes internationally and specializes in a particular industry or function. It may recruit at a senior level of management within its niche, and it may also take assignments at the middle-management level, again within its area of specialization. Either of these types of firms can be retained or contingency.

How do you choose which type of firm with which to work? How do you know if the boutique firm can provide the same level of service as the multi-office, multinational giants? And how about individual recruiters with little or no staff? Where do they fit into the mix? Depending upon your career goals, global firms, boutique firms, and individual recruiters may all serve your needs! You need to closely examine your objectives, determine what industry or industries you want to focus on, what level of management you are at today and where you want to be in the future, what your functional expertise is, and what your geographic preferences are. Given these parameters, the size of the firm may be less important to your career navigation than industry or functional specialization. In fact, typically the boutique firms have more contacts and greater expertise in their niche than the global firms. This definitely is an area in which you need to do your homework to make the determination as to what type of firm best serves your needs.

Let's take a look at a profile of Korn/Ferry International as an example of a global firm. According to Hunt-Scanlon's *Executive Recruiters of North America 2000* and *Executive Search Review,* Korn/Ferry International, founded in 1969, is the largest U.S. executive search firm. Korn/Ferry is a generalist firm that recruits senior-level management for the advanced technology, aerospace/defense, board services, consumer products, corporate communications, education, energy, entertainment, fashion (retail/apparel), financial services, health care/hospitals, information technology, insurance, nonprofit, pharmaceutical/medical, physician/executive, professional services, provider/managed health care, and real estate industries, among others. The firm's practice is international in scope and currently includes 298 executive recruiters based in 22 offices in cities across the United States, Canada, and Mexico. Its international branch offices are in 48 cities outside North America. Salary minimum for assignments is $100,000.

If you are a middle-management executive with a goal to become a senior-level line manager and potentially progress to the CEO level and/or arc seeking a seat on a board of directors, this type of search firm will likely be the one you want to target. However, there are some issues of which you need to be aware when you commit to this option. The larger search firms may appear or attempt to be all things to all constituencies (both client companies and prospective candidates) and lack depth in specific industries or functions. Remember, their practices are competing with niche players that have emerged and have deeper expertise in industries or functions, such as financial services, health care, training, high tech, communications, and so on. In fact, some of the large search firms oftentimes charge clients additional fees beyond the 33.3 percent of the first-year cash compensation— up to 50 percent and higher—for areas in which they lack expertise. Why would a client want to pay more when he could work with a specialist firm, have lower fees, and most likely garner better results? Often a smaller firm can provide better service to both client and candidate, and with an equal or lesser fee.

Handcuffs of Their Own Design— The Reality Check Hits Home

Another issue to consider is conflict of interest, or "off-limits policy." This is a key issue in executive search, particularly with the global search firms. An off-limits policy refers to a search firm agreeing not to approach executives in their clients' organizations. This policy can apply to a restricted period of time and/or restrictions within the entire corporation or could possibly be only limited to a division of the client company. The off-limits policy becomes a critical issue when the field of potential candidates is limited to a client's major competitors. If a large search firm has worked for all of those companies, where will it find the best candidates? Most important to you is the fact that with such obvious limitations, it may also mean that *you*—the candidate—can't compete for opportunities represented by the global firms because you might currently work for one of their client companies! Some firms may not divulge the off-limits issue to their clients, as it clearly reduces the universe of candidates from which they can recruit. This becomes an ethical question that some firms might sidestep in discussing the search process with their clients.

Conversely, the smaller search firms usually do not face the issue of conflict of interest because the volume of searches is not as great and they typically specialize in either one industry conducting search in multiple disciplines or focus on two or three related functions working across nearly all industries.

The bottom line: When targeting either global or boutique firms, you need to conduct extensive research on both types and determine which can be most productive, most nimble, and best suited to helping you reach your intended objectives given your area of expertise and career goals.

Industry Specialization versus Functional Discipline

As you conduct your research into the search firm or recruiter that best serves your needs, it will be helpful to your identification effort to know that in addition to the types of recruiters we discussed in Chapter 2, executive search firms also are categorized by industry specialization and functional discipline.

An executive position consists of carrying out a function, and it most often takes place within a specific industry. For example, a particular position might be focused on the marketing function and be in a health care industry company. Another position may focus on the function of plant management in the automotive industry. Industry and function are other areas on which you should focus to help you cull the recruiters you want to target and determine those best suited to your career goals. Depending upon your area of expertise, you may wish to target search firms that specialize in both the particular function and industry in which you have experience. Or if your career path has provided you the opportunity to perform various functions within one industry, you may be ready to consider new industries.

Although most of the large search firms are labeled as generalist firms because they place executives in almost all functional disciplines and industries, they are often comprised of several specialty practice areas, typically with an industry focus such as manufacturing, financial services, high technology, health care, and so on. Some firms also divide their practices functionally as well into categories such as general management, sales and marketing, research and development, and other such functions. As I mentioned earlier, there are many boutique firms that specialize in a particular industry or industries and function or functions. Depending upon your career goals, you will need to look within yourself as well as conduct research to determine which type of firm best serves your particular needs.

Gauging a Firm's Reputation and Cultural Fit with You

Although directories of executive search firms, Web sites, and other such resources can provide you with comprehensive lists of recruiters, complete with names, titles, addresses, phone and fax numbers, and e-mail addresses, what they cannot do for you is gauge their reputation. Neither can they assess cultural fit—or more simply put, the simpatico factor—with you as a candidate. Remember, value structure and cultural fit between the recruiter and candidate *are* a critical factor in the partnership you will hopefully develop with many recruiters. Only you can determine that through your own diligent efforts.

Further, even search firms' and recruiters' Web sites may not give you an accurate, honest portrayal of their own standing in the profession. You *must* conduct the research yourself to ensure you are working with a reputable search firm/recruiter. It is critical that you know in whose hands you are putting your future.

But where do you begin in conducting this research, and what questions should you ask? Here's my list of 10 resources to contact or investigate and 10 questions to ask or focus on during your research. As you speak with or review information from these resources, ask as many questions as you can. Be inquisitive. Your innate curiosity, ingenuity, and perseverance will get you further than most.

10 Best Resources to Contact/Investigate

1. **Professional mentors, peers and colleagues.** When you seek advice from this group of professionals about which firm or recruiter to target, ask them the following list of questions; if they answer positively, you should feel pretty comfortable with their recommendation.
2. **College career centers or alumni organizations/job fairs.** Although these groups may know about the reputable firms, the firms they recommend may be for entry- or lower-level executives.
3. **Professional organizations and associations, particularly those in which you are a member.** These groups may be the best resources, as their members

have likely had significant experience in hiring executive search firms themselves and in working with them as candidates.

4. **The Internet.** Investigate posted articles, community news groups, career chat rooms, and Web sites; for publicly traded firms, information is available through the Security Exchange Commission's site and other public disclosure sites.

5. **Newspapers, magazines, and other journals and publications.** These are available either online or archived in libraries, colleges, and bookstores. Check as many publications as possible to properly gauge reputation.

6. **Company human resource departments or employees.** This may seem like a bold step, but contacting human resource representatives or employees at companies that you respect and may be targeting for employment can be a tremendous help when you approach them with candor and respect for their time.

7. **Search firms' or recruiters' client references.** If you have targeted the firms you wish to contact, call them and ask for a brochure or visit their Web site, and then get a list of their clients. Contact the clients directly and seek someone who can speak about their experience in working with the firm.

8. **Personal mentors and social organizations.** Although likely to not garner the same quantity or quality of leads you may want in seeking information on headhunters' reputation as professional mentors or organizations, these personal and social contacts may nonetheless give you some good insight.

9. **Other search firms and headhunters.** If you have found a search firm that you believe is reputable but may not have assignments in your area of expertise or industry, ask the recruiters with the firm whom they might recommend as a reputable firm best suited to your goals.

10. **Vendors who work with the organization.** These may be difficult to identify. However, if you find a vendor, such as an outplacement firm, relocation firm, or background-checking organization, ask about the reputation of the firm, how respectful the firm was to them as a vendor, and if they would be comfortable recommending them to you.

Top 10 Challenging Questions Inquiring Professionals Must Seek to Answer

1. How long has the firm/recruiter been in business?
2. What is the recruiter's background prior to executive search?
3. For what companies has the recruiter conducted search?
4. Of the searches she conducts annually, how many has she completed successfully? And how many have derailed and why?
5. Was the client base treated well by the recruiter and its staff?
6. Did the recruiters have in-depth knowledge of the search profession and process as well as the industry and function in which they worked on the client's behalf?
7. Is repeat business with the firm a foregone conclusion?
8. How is the firm and the recruiter perceived by their peers? By industry/function contacts? What does the respect meter read?
9. Was superior counseling a part of its modus operandi? Or was it a body broker in disguise?
10. What were the toughest challenges the recruiter faced with a candidate?

So now you've done your research and have identified a list of recruiters that you believe are most suited to your career goals ... what's next? How do you attract the recruiter's attention, and what can you expect from that relationship? When is it appropriate for you to make the call to the headhunter, and when is it most likely that the recruiter will call you? We'll explore all the answers to these mysteries in the next chapter.

———

Secret: It's time to turn the tables on the executive search profession—identify and qualify the recruiters. Be just as precise, thorough, and seemingly competent as they attempt to be with you. After all, it's *your career, not theirs!*

CHAPTER 4

The Chicken or the Egg... Who Makes the First Contact, You or the Recruiter?

When Does the Recruiter Enter Your Life?

For those of you who have had experience working with a recruiter, you have probably reached certain milestones in your career that have made you an attractive candidate—and you recognize what those milestones are. If you have never dealt with a recruiter, it may be a mystery to you as to what point in your career a recruiter should enter your life, what it takes to attract the attention of a recruiter, and how to leverage that relationship to move your career to a higher level. So just when *does* the recruiter enter your life?

The most basic fact about when a recruiter should or should not enter your life has to do with your own readiness to move your career forward. However, even if you are not ready to make a job change, there are fundamental ways to launch the dialogue with a recruiter and begin building what will be one of the most critical relationships in your career navigation efforts and the duration of your professional life. What does it take to attract a recruiter's attention? Let's take a look at five key components that will improve your chances of registering on the recruiter's radar screen.

Life's Always a Two-Way Street— Add Value beyond Simply Being a Potential Candidate

Critical to the success of developing and maintaining your relationship with a recruiter is to recognize that as the professional being contacted by a search firm, you serve in a dual capacity—as potential candidate for a specific position and/or as a source of other candidates for that position. Regardless of which role you serve, your positive interaction with an executive search professional will be one of the smartest survival strategies available in today's competitive marketplace.

Taking charge in this relationship can mean a variety of things to both sides of the equation. On your side, when a recruiter calls, you should be prompt in responding and demonstrate some interest in engaging in an open, free-flowing exchange of thoughts and ideas. The conversation should explore everything from inquiring about the recruiter's firm (especially if it is unknown to you) and learning more about the recruiter's own background and experience in the executive search arena to listening thoughtfully to the details of his or her current search.

In most instances, a recruiter will be calling to inquire whether you are interested in a specific search that he or she is conducting. Some calls may pique your interest, and others may not. The most important factor to remember is that you must convey to the search professional *precisely* what your career aspirations are and aren't. To accomplish that, you should take charge and outline your own parameters and limitations as a candidate without being concerned that there will be any negative repercussions at all. You *must* be candid and communicate directly and honestly. With this posture on your part, the relationship will evolve into one that is truly meaningful to both you and the search professional.

Should you decide that the opportunity the recruiter has described is not for you, don't feel sheepish about indicating that it is not quite what you believe would be your best next career step. More important, take advantage of the opportunity to shift your role in the relationship. At this point in the conversation, you now have the potential to become, in the mind of the recruiter, a valuable source of candidates for his or her search. As a result, listen even more carefully to the specific details about the position and volunteer to refer professionals whom you deem highly qualified for it.

Now let's address that very subject of referring candidates, or being a source of, candidates. It is critical for a recruiter to develop a network of trusted sources of candidates to have a successful executive search practice. Developing relationships with these sources is truly the lifeblood of a search firm's existence. Its sources are where the firm obtains a significant number of candidate contacts as well as prospective client leads. You might reason that surely a search firm must obtain names of potential candidates from lists of executive contacts that just about anyone can purchase from companies that sell these names from vast databases. And another way a search firm can obtain names is by simply joining a professional organization and marketing to its membership list, which is highly unprofessional. However, in reality identifying professionals is not this easy. If it were, you would see far more headhunters in the world than those in existence today.

The best candidate contacts are often generated by recruiters' trusted sources. And establishing yourself as a credible source of candidates is an excellent way to develop and nurture a solid relationship with members of the executive search community. However, remember that everything you say and do will reflect significantly on the recruiter's perception of your value as a source of candidates—and, more significantly, on his or her perception of you in general as a professional. Consequently, make sure that you do not recommend individuals of mediocre talent or who only meet a few of the recruiter's criteria for the position. Only mention those you consider as "best in class" within your specific profession. A recruiter would much rather that you not refer any candidates than to have you recommend ones that will only waste his or her time. Poor referrals reflect negatively on your evaluative skills and your ability to make sound, objective judgment calls.

Make Yourself a Known Entity to the Recruitment Community

When your circumstances are such that you are content with your current situation and your career track, you may not feel the need to make yourself known to recruiters. After all, you've gotten to this point in your professional life without their help—why would you need them now? Don't bury your head in the sand! There are no guarantees that the job you have today will be there tomorrow, no matter how happy your employer is with your performance or how successful your company is, particularly in today's employment market and our fast-changing business and organizational models.

In fact, your position as it is structured today may not even exist tomorrow. In a recent issue of *Time* magazine, Tom Peters, a world-renowned management consultant, stated: "I believe that 90% of white-collar jobs in the U.S. will either be destroyed or altered beyond recognition in the next 10 to 15 years. That's a catastrophic prediction given that 90% of us are engaged in white-collar work of one sort or another. . . .

The productivity tool kit aims to reconstruct—make that deconstruct—the white-collar world." His words should shoot ice water into the veins of those who are confident that their current employment situation is secure. Although it's perfectly fine to be happy in one's position at a company, it is in your best interest to always keep your options open and to be receptive to recruiters' overtures.

With that made clear, let's return to the subject of how to make yourself known to the recruitment community. One point I want to make before we address the how is to address the why. *Why* should you go to any effort to become known to recruiters? Shouldn't they be finding you? One way to look at this is by putting yourself in the shoes of the recruiter. In the first chapter, I described what my typical week looked like. Recruiters, without question, have a 24/7 work life. And it's focused primarily at finding and qualifying candidates. Although significant potential candidate contacts are made through a recruiter's trusted sources, researching new candidates through other means is still a considerable, time-consuming part of the search process. It's to your benefit to make the recruiter's job easier to find you. *Raise your profile in the business world.* Here are some suggestions for increasing your visibility among recruiters as well as the professionals that may suggest you as a potential candidate to recruiters:

- Join industry associations and professional organizations and become an active member—in other words, network!
- Initiate speaking engagements in forums appropriate and relevant to your profession or industry. Be viewed as a cutting-edge thought leader.
- Write articles in industry trade and professional publications or other such journals, and if and when published, send the articles to recruiters and professional contacts you feel might serve to advance your career.
- Become well known to coworkers both within and outside your department by taking the initiative on

high-visibility projects as well as supporting colleagues in their endeavors.

- Be active in your community. Support nonprofit organizations relevant to your work and participate in fund-raising activities and events.
- Send your resume to a targeted list of recruiters. Although this may seem an obvious tactic, individuals who are not looking to make a change don't always think to send a resume to recruiters until they are desperate. Be proactive. Don't wait until you need a job to make yourself known to recruiters.

It is important to recognize that although reputable recruiters are not looking for the easy way out in their approach to identifying candidates, time is of the essence in today's "want-it-now" corporate environment. Let's look at a couple of scenarios of how making yourself visible in the business world will benefit your career navigation.

A recruiter is waiting for a plane to depart and is perusing through a stack of catch-up reading he brought along on the flight. He comes across a particularly thought-provoking article that you wrote. You happen to be a CFO with a mid-sized manufacturing company. He is currently conducting a search for a CFO for a major manufacturing company. He likes your opinions and strategic thinking. You are brilliant, in his estimation. Your personality even comes through in the article. Wow, he thinks, why don't I know this professional? Well, now he does. It is very likely that he will contact you on this trip to see if you may be interested in the opportunity for which he seeking candidates. If you are not interested this time, you can bet that your contact information will be included in the firm's database of candidates for future opportunities.

Another scenario: A recruiter is attending an industry association's annual awards dinner. You are a member of this organization and are viewed as an up-and-coming thought leader among the group. You are chosen as a keynote speaker. Your lively and appropriately humorous remarks impress the recruiter. She currently is conducting a search for a sales manager in your industry, and she finds your presentation style to be precisely on target for the position. She will approach you at the end of the awards dinner and set up a time for the two of you to meet. Had you only sent a resume to the recruiter in the past, it might have been overlooked. The opportunity to be seen and heard in this type of forum is invaluable for your career navigation.

Although you may not be seeking a change when the recruiter approaches you, when you are ready for your next move, you will have already increased your visibility in the search community, which will prove far more fruitful than you ever could have imagined.

Present Yourself in a Credible Manner

Although you can make your best effort to become known through the methods I suggested in the previous section, understanding how the executive search profession defines its community of professionals deemed worthy of contacting (otherwise known as the "radar screen") is exceedingly difficult. In reality, there is no commonality or consistency from one search firm to another in terms of who qualifies to be on the radar screen and who does not. As a result, the process of distinguishing oneself with the recruitment profession has become, oftentimes, an overwhelming task to contemplate. However, in my view, one overriding factor will set apart any professional as far as career navigation is concerned and as far as making it onto the radar screens of small and large search firms. It's simple. Focus on *best practices* in every contribution that you make in your current position, in your overall profession, and in the counsel that you provide to your subordinates, peers, and senior management. The reality is that in today's employment jungle, corporations are seeking to hire those who exceed expectations and those who channel their energies into producing exceptional results!

So you have made your mark in your current position and have received recognition from senior management through promotions, raises, a company car, and your own office. How do you convey your achievements to executive recruiters? Essentially, if you truly are a stellar performer in your chosen profession, it is very likely that you will come to our attention because if you have focused on the notion of best practices in all you do, you will probably be referred to us by several individuals who have had professional contact with you; you most likely will be the one making thought-provoking remarks at the podium, and you will no doubt have authored the articles that present you as a leader in your industry or function—all of which lead to getting yourself on recruiters' radar screens.

If you realize that you are not quite at the level in your career to be making speeches or writing authoritative articles and your resume is pretty much the sole vehicle to demonstrate your capabilities, be sure to bring forth all of your accomplishments in this document—not only your responsibilities. Identify what value you brought to a company's growth or other corporate objectives. Tout your successes and how you achieved them. Demonstrate the results of your efforts rather than the mere fact that you made the effort. (I'll discuss more about writing an impactful resume in my chapter on branding your career.) It's all in how you package your career.

Packaging the Milestones

Speaking of packaging your career, it is critical for you to recognize the milestones in your professional life and how to package them for presentation. Whether you are writing a resume or preparing for a live interview, these milestones provide recruiters with the substantive information they need to judge whether to make initial contact with you for a search they are conducting now or in the future. It's all about distinguishing yourself from the hundreds of other potential candidates whom recruiters encounter daily. If your resume and personal presentation is a bland glimpse of your work history, then there is no compelling evidence to prompt a recruiter to move you forward in the process.

What are the milestones recruiters typically look for, and how do you package them? Essentially, we're looking for how you have navigated your career up to the present time and the highlights of your experiences and accomplishments along that path. This would include your education—academic degrees as well as honors and other credentials earned and whether you financed your own education, how you secured your first job and subsequent positions and the circumstances under which you left each position—particularly a promotion or recruitment to a more senior-level post, and your accomplishments in each position—how you added value to the organization and helped a company meet or exceed its business objectives.

Other milestones we may look for in your career progression include moving successfully from one industry or functional discipline to another; being the first in your company or department to achieve a specified goal, undertake a certain project, or secure an appointment to a newly created post; a change in reporting structure resulting in your reporting to a more senior-level executive in the organization; cross-functional accomplishments that demonstrate your ability to perform well across the silos as a strong utility player as well as showing your teamwork, and other such notables in your career. You may also wish to discuss how you overcame obstacles in moving your career forward, such as launching your own consultancy after being laid off during a downturn in the economy or other such feats that demonstrate your proactive, glass-half-full positive mentality. These qualities score high with recruiters.

Be Confident in Your Qualifications— Pedigree versus Junkyard Dog Theory

You may ask yourself, am I qualified to be contacted by an executive recruiter? Do I need a slate of academic degrees to be considered a candidate for the positions they are seeking to fill? Let me clear up any mysteries for you as to whom I view as the best candidate profile for our assignments. I've long characterized the world by dividing people into two groups, which frankly have nothing to do with economic or social status or academic degrees. I call it the "pedigree versus junkyard dog" theory. The pedigrees more often than not are defined by their entitlement mentality, lack of interest in getting their fingernails dirty, and their "there but for the grace of God go I" perspective on life. The junkyard dogs, however, are truly the most fascinating and intriguing of the two categories. Junkyard dogs exude tenacity and self-confidence and are risk takers focused on achieving beyond the end goal. The junkyard dog also is an innately curious type of individual whose own desire for knowledge allows her to creep into corners of life where the pedigrees aren't allowed to go. So when you look at the world of professionals in an attempt to predict who in the end will be the most successful, one immediately senses and feels the power of the junkyard dogs.

For those of you who need further explanation of how I define *pedigree*, consider those professionals whose careers have happened upon them and have been privileged only by working for blue-chip, multinational corporations and then contrast them with the following real-life example of how I witnessed the junkyard-dog profile succeed. I presented to a top global technology corporation a candidate who was similar to the dark horse in a race. He, of course, had all of the technical skills he needed to succeed in the job; however, he had none of the glaring, obvious high-profile pedigree positions in his career or academic degrees that would make him a slam-dunk, top-choice candidate for a client. However, his blend of tenacity, intellectual curiosity, risk tolerance, and quietly earned achievements sparked immediate interest on the part of the client after only a single round of interviews. And, by the way, he was an unknown and was not on the radar screen of most search firms. He was a professional whose career had not taken the obvious well-known path with which many hiring executives are familiar; rather, he had taken a less traditional route to success. Nonetheless, he far exceeded expectations as a result of the significant intangible attributes he had as an individual. I believe that these core competencies, or intangible attributes, are far more important for a candidate to possess than the technical skills or academic degrees he brings to the table. These intangible qualities are so critical to success that I've dedicated an entire chapter to them so that you will thoroughly understand what those are, how to recognize them in yourself, and how to leverage them as you navigate your career.

The Big Debate—When Do You Call a Recruiter?

So back to the chicken-and-the-egg issue—do you make the first call to the recruiter, or is it more appropriate to wait for the recruiter to call you? How do you recognize that fateful moment in time when you should make the call to the recruiter? There are basically two choices in the matter: Wait until you are desperate to leave your current position, or take a proactive approach and build solid relationships with your recruitment contacts *long before you need them*. Which do you think is the better approach? Although the answer may appear obvious, you'd be surprised at how many individuals don't even think about taking the proactive approach and contacting a recruiter first. Waiting until you are completely dissatisfied with your current job is not the wisest way to navigate a relationship with an executive search professional. When layoffs are impending at your company or a colleague gets the promotion that you thought you had earned or your department's budget gets slashed, you should not wait until you're ready to quit before you think about developing a relationship with the executive search community.

Similarly, throwing yourself into every search that comes your way can result in the same loss in credibility with the recruitment profession. The first approach puts you in the compromising position of having to lower your expectations about the quality of the opportunity you consider, because you are so desperately unhappy in your current situation. The second, shopping the possibilities, if you will, positions you as a professional who is indecisive, possibly looking to leverage another company's potential interest in your talent as a means of either validating your own worth or as a means to garnering higher compensation with your current employer via the threat of taking another position. You gain nothing from employing either of these approaches. In fact, you lose credibility with the search community, and eventually the calls from recruiters will stop coming.

One of the most important points to remember is that as recruiters, we are constantly assessing the professional's frame of mind. Our clients retain us to determine the mind-set of all the candidates whom we deem qualified for a specific position. Given that premise, remember that when you interact with a recruiter, your mind-set is critical to the relationship that you will develop and evolve with us. The most important advice that I can offer you is to be proactive, to engage in a two-way exchange of thoughts and ideas, and not to wait until your present position becomes tenuous or untenable before you approach the executive search community.

When is it more appropriate for you to wait until the recruiter contacts you? Rarely. Although you don't want to be overly aggressive in your overtures to recruiters, waiting for the recruiter to call you to discuss a position is poor judgment. You may be the ideal candidate for a recruiter's assignment, but he may not contact you for a variety of reasons: (1) Your contact information is outdated and the recruiter cannot find you; (2) a recruiter's database contains many thousands of contacts, and even if the recruiter has placed your name in the database, there may be a technical problem in retrieving it; (3) a recruiter meets hundreds of candidates each year, and if you haven't remained in contact, you may be supplanted in his memory by candidates who are top of mind; or (4) the recruiter may not know or recall that your background includes expertise in the discipline of the position he is seeking to fill—you may have been approached by the recruiter for a position with a different focus, and that's how he remembers you.

In short, there are a variety of reasons a recruiter may *not* call you, so it is in your best interest to contact a recruiter and develop a relationship with an individual whose role in the corporate arena will bring you what may be your next best career move. So, even if a recruiter is calling you to solicit names of candidates for a particular search she is conducting, view the interaction as an opportunity, not an annoyance. Nearly every call and every contact you have with a recruiter can be beneficial to you in the near term *and* the long term.

Do the Rules Change for Profession- or Function-Specific Opportunities?

There may be professions or functional disciplines in which you believe it's best or indeed more appropriate for you to sit back and let the recruiter make the first contact. Not so. In today's hiring markets, all traditional rules of the past have evaporated. Whether you are a physician, attorney, CEO, accountant, or marketing professional, don't wait for the recruiter to come knocking on your door. You may feel that you are too busy or that because of your high profile you don't need to make contact with recruiters—you have a "let them find me" mentality. Wrong approach. Remember two points: First, it is a career death wish to wait to contact the executive search community until you are desperate to find a job. You may find yourself left out in the cold with recruiters, as relationship building is critical with this group. And second, never assume the recruiter can find you, no matter how successful you have become in your career. If you fear jeopardizing your current position by contacting a headhunter, remember that the risk of disclosure when you work with reputable search firms is minimal.

A recruiter who may know your immediate supervisor and disclose to her the fact that you just called his search firm would serve no purpose, and if a recruiter continued to divulge such confidences, the individual would be put out of business fast. After all, if your immediate supervisor who received the call from the recruiter has also been a candidate with this recruiter, do you think she would feel comfortable working with this person again, knowing he might reveal his or her confidential information as well? A recruiter who participates in such gossipy activity is either desperate for a placement and/or will have no credibility in the marketplace.

So, what's the best way to work with a recruiter? Let's explore that in the next chapter.

———

Secret: Reality check—Recruiters don't just enter your life, they barge into it hoping that you are going to let them "own" you. I say, barge right back into their world! After all, they need you more in today's hiring market than you may need them.

CHAPTER **5**

The Mechanics of Working with a Recruiter
How Does It All Work?

Now that I have dispelled some of the mysteries of executive search in the past three chapters and you've learned more about the nature of what headhunters do for a living, the various types of recruiters, and how and when to get the attention of recruiters—what comes next? What do you do with them once you've engaged them? What should you say? What shouldn't you say? How should you behave? What results can you expect from working with a recruiter? How can you ensure that you gain the most from every interaction with this professional? The bottom line is that every call and every interaction you have with a recruiter should be a positive experience and beneficial to you either now or in the future. Whether you—the candidate—or the recruiter makes the initial contact, it will work to your benefit to understand the mechanics of working with a recruiter so as to maximize the advantages to both parties.

If you are working with either a retained or contingency recruiter, you need to understand some basic fundamentals to ensure a positive experience and to improve your chances of securing a job interview. This is your opportunity to develop and build a relationship with an individual who, hopefully, will bring you your next best career step. Essentially, most recruiters are interested in engaging a prospective candidate in an earnest conversation that will enable them to become more familiar with that individual's career and with his or her future career goals. In this and the following chapter, I'll share with you some of the inner workings of the search process and how best to leverage your relationship with a recruiter so that you may optimize your career navigation efforts.

Engaging in a Relationship with an Executive Recruiter

Suppose you are a bright, capable, up-and-coming midlevel management executive. You feel confident that you know the workings of the day-to-day business world, and you feel you know your job so well that you are ready to burst out of its confines and move up to the next level of management. And you may be at that certain point in your career where you will have had exposure to executive recruiters. In fact, they may contact you on a fairly regularly basis, and you may already feel comfortable that you know the drill—that you know everything there is to know about working with a headhunter from your few experiences. Not so. At the less-than-senior executive level in your career, the search professional with whom you worked may have been a contingency recruiter, a junior member of a retained firm, a sole practitioner, a research-level recruiter, or perhaps even an employment agency representative. You can't be expected to know the difference among these recruiters from your limited interaction with them, let alone how best to work with them.

You've been focused on your daily responsibilities at work and making your mark within your organization, and navigating your career with a headhunter hasn't been particularly important to you. Until now.

Now you recognize that people around you have moved up or moved on in their career, and most have likely done so through the efforts of an executive recruiter. That's how it works. There are few professionals who have changed jobs at the mid- to senior-level management stage of their career without working with a recruiter. In fact, according to Kennedy Information Online, a recent study by Coopers & Lybrand found that 64 percent of executive positions are filled through recruiters. Your challenge: figuring out how to become part of this statistic! There are various ways to initiate a relationship with a recruiter, as I discussed in the previous chapter. There are times the recruiter may call you, and other times when you may contact the recruiter. Now I'd like to share with you—step by step—how you enter this supposed inner sanctum of executive recruiting. You need to know what to expect during the search process at this phase of your career navigation as you will likely be contacted by a retained recruiter, and although each may operate somewhat differently from the next, their methods will be similar enough so you will know what part you play at each step. To better familiarize you with the process, I have developed and copyrighted The Recruitment Cycle chart (Figure 5.1), which describes the process my firm employs in conducting search. Let me walk you through the steps shown in this chart and then describe to you how and when you become a part of the process.

Figure 5.1 The Recruitment Cycle.

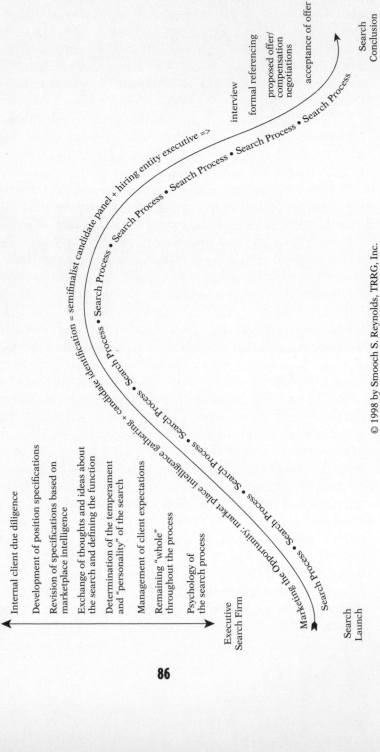

Client Corporation
(Hiring Executive)

Internal client due diligence

Development of position specifications

Revision of specifications based on marketplace intelligence

Exchange of thoughts and ideas about the search and defining the function

Determination of the temperament and "personality" of the search

Management of client expectations

Remaining "whole" throughout the process

Psychology of the search process

Executive Search Firm

Marketing the Opportunity: market place intelligence gathering + candidate identification = semifinalist candidate panel + hiring entity executive =>

Marketing the Opportunity • Search Process • Search Process • Search Process • Search Process • Search Process • Search Process • Search Process • Search Process • Search Process • Search Process • Search Process • Search Process • Search Process

interview

formal referencing

proposed offer/compensation negotiations

acceptance of offer

Search Conclusion

Search Launch

© 1998 by Smooch S. Reynolds, TRRG, Inc.

86

Beginning the Search Process—Internal Client Due Diligence; Development of the Position Description

As I pointed out in Chapter 1, the first phase in the process of a retained search after we have secured a new client involves discussing our philosophy of search and outlining for the client hiring executives how the search process happens. We also will conduct a thorough client briefing, or due diligence session. During this conference, we define the search assignment as well as gain a better understanding of the organization's corporate culture. We conduct in-depth interviews with our client contacts to determine precisely the temperament or personality of the organization and the expectations of its executives prior to launching the search.

Following this meeting, we create a position description outlining the parameters of the position's responsibilities as well as the experience and characteristics needed for the candidate to be successful in the role. We also will establish a range for the position's compensation (annual base salary, percent annual target bonus, and whether the position is stock option eligible) as well as any other benefits and perquisites associated with the opportunity. Combining the information we glean from this meeting with our own research will enable us to produce an extensive position description. We use this position description to send to candidates we target as well as key sources who may help us to identify candidates.

During this initial phase of the search process, we are not aggressively contacting candidates, although we may contact key sources in the marketplace to begin our strategy to market the opportunity. In these early stages of the search, the recruiter will be scanning his or her mental Rolodex, but until the position specifications are agreed upon by the client and the search firm, the recruiter will not begin our search efforts in earnest, although we will begin the behind-the-scenes research that prepares us for the outreach into the potential candidate pool. This is the part of search that you will never see. Our research involves evaluating the marketplace, identifying companies to target as sources of candidates, and generating lists of potential candidates and sources from our own in-house database of contacts. Once this research is well underway (and it does not stop until the close of the search), we will begin marketing the assignment.

Marketing the Opportunity/Research/ Marketplace Intelligence Gathering/ Candidate Identification

This next phase of the search process is where we officially launch the search and market the opportunity throughout the geographic region appropriate to the search. As you can see on my chart, it is the most significant segment and most time-intensive portion of this process. This phase is where we cast the net broadly to our network of contacts and begin discussing the opportunity with both potential candidates and sources of candidates. During this portion of the search, we gather marketplace intelligence gleaned from speaking with our contacts, who share with us what they think about the opportunity, both the pluses and minuses. Marketplace intelligence might include hurdles we must address and overcome in marketing the opportunity, such as problems with the company's business model, management reputation, or corporate culture; issues with the position title, compensation, or reporting structure; or an issue seemingly as simple as the location of the company's headquarters. As a valued contact of the search professional, the marketplace information you provide the headhunter can be invaluable to the shaping of the position and the search process in general. Without disclosing our sources, we share this feedback with the client and advise them of the hurdles we are encountering in moving the search forward. Not every search firm takes this step, but we believe in providing forthright and thorough counsel to our clients, and we also believe it is our responsibility to advise them of the hurdles and how they might be overcome. Although it may seem fundamental, information gleaned from our research helps us further shape the parameters of the position as the search progresses and aids us in the candidate identification process. This information can also assist our clients in solving internal problems they were unaware of until this point.

It is during this phase of the search that you will most likely be contacted either as a source of candidates or as a potential candidate yourself. Let's see how this might unfold during the search process.

Getting to Know You—The Courtesy Interview

One of your first encounters with an executive recruiter may be via the courtesy interview. The lifeblood of headhunters is their database of professional contacts. Recruiters are forever seeking new, qualified candidates to get to know and whom they may potentially present to their clients. How do you get a courtesy interview with a search professional? Is it as simple as calling the firm and scheduling a time to meet? Do you just send your resume and hope for the best? Or does the recruiter find you? It's slightly different among the different types of recruiters. Contingency recruiters—who likely will not have a retained search—will welcome courtesy interviews, as the more individuals they meet, the more chances they have to shop you around to potential clients in hopes of a placement. On the other hand, the retained recruiter who is representing the client has a limited amount of time and may not be as available for a courtesy interview as his or her contingency cousin. Yet courtesy interviews can still be an important part of the overall candidate identification process for retained search professionals.

You will most likely be contacted for a courtesy interview—usually to be conducted by the recruiter on the telephone—

for one of three reasons: (1) You were referred to the recruiter by a respected contact (either a source, former candidate, or client) as someone she should get to know as a potential candidate for future searches; (2) the recruiter saw your name mentioned in an article, or she met you at a business function and felt you could be a potential candidate; or (3) you sent your resume to a search firm, and a recruiter thought you might be qualified for future assignments and wanted to get to know you better for that eventuality. The retained recruiter may only schedule a telephone interview with you that might take only 15 or 20 minutes of her time. That is because the recruiter is working within tight time constraints to identify candidates that meet qualifications for the assignments she currently has. Let's say the recruiter has five great candidates for an assignment, and your name is given to her as someone she should get to know. What's the motivation for the recruiter to present one more candidate to the client when she already has a full slate, or panel, of candidates? With very limited time at hand when conducting perhaps 8 to 12 searches at once (you'll recall from Chapter 1 the week in my life as an executive recruiter), she may put your information aside for a period of time and get back to it when she can spare 15 minutes.

What can you expect from a courtesy interview with a search professional? At this point in your discussions with a recruiter, she usually just wants a general snapshot of your work history and a sense of your accomplishments as well as an assessment of your overall professional demeanor/ presentation style (which should be determined in person). In addition, the search professional will want to know why you may be considering seeking a change in employment, whether you can relocate domestically and/or internationally, and the components of your current compensation. This information, combined with what you provide in your resume, will give the recruiter enough about your experience and background to assess whether you may be a viable potential candidate for future assignments. If so, your information will be included in the search firm's database of contacts, and you may be contacted by this recruiter or other professionals in the firm. Or you may not. It all depends on the type of assignments the firm has.

At best, if you have made a strong impression upon the recruiter, you will have an opportunity to be contacted by the search firm in the future. If it is a reputable retained search firm, that's not a bad situation to be in—after all, your goal is to begin and evolve a long-term relationship with this new career advocate. Optimally, if you are ready for a change and your background proves to be suited for an assignment where the recruiter does *not* have a panel of candidates, you may be fully qualified for a search he is conducting and, after a series of additional steps, which I will also discuss in this chapter, you may be presented to the client company as a candidate. So the courtesy interview is beneficial to you as well as the recruiter.

Candidate or Source? The Exploratory Telephone Interview

A significant part of the research that a recruiter conducts is outreach via the telephone. In addition to the courtesy interview, another way you may be introduced to the search process is through an exploratory telephone interview. The goal of the recruiter is to determine if you are a viable candidate (or a source of candidates) for an opportunity. In this scenario, a recruiter has a list of contacts before him. This list may have been generated from the search firm's database and supplemented by a list generated from additional research of contacts gleaned from company Web sites, professional organizations' membership lists, newspapers, magazines, and a host of other such resources. How many names might appear on this list? Maybe three hundred to five hundred. Possibly more, possibly less. The recruiter's ultimate goal is to cull this list to a panel of semifinalist candidates to present to the hiring executives at the client company. How many candidates will be on the panel? Optimally, between four and six semifinalists. Any more than that may be confusing to the client; any fewer may prove not enough for the hiring executive to make a well-informed decision. Clearly, recruiters have their work cut out for them!

The recruiter will not call every name on the list. His job is to examine the list and identify those individuals he wishes to target as potential candidates or sources of candidates. Suppose your name, title, company, and work telephone number appear on this list. He will determine from this limited information which category you might fit—potential candidate or source. If your contact information was generated from the firm's database, there may be additional information on your background from a prior courtesy interview, or you may have been a candidate or source from prior searches. The recruiter will review this information and decide whether or not he will contact you for one of the assignments.

The search professional may initially contact you as a source of candidates, inquiring as to whether or not you might refer an individual who may be qualified for a search she is conducting for a specific position or positions. You know the recruiter and feel comfortable referring candidates. If you don't know the recruiter or the search firm, don't feel obligated to respond. When you are first contacted, you may ask the recruiter about the firm—particularly whether or not it is retained or contingency—and tell her you'll return the call later. If you do some research and see this is a legitimate search with a reputable firm, you may feel comfortable referring candidates. If not, never refer your contacts to a firm that does not have a solid reputation or is unknown within the search community or your industry or by functional contacts (refer to "Gauging a Firm's Reputation and Cultural Fit With You" in Chapter 3). Your contacts will not appreciate your doing so and it serves you no purpose, as the search firm will not be one you will wish to interact with again. If you decide to refer potential candidates to the firm, you may wish to contact them first prior to giving even a reputable recruiter their information. Or you may already know that your contacts are willing to have their name given to a recruiter. The recruiter may then call some or all of your referrals and will initiate a dialogue with them about the opportunity.

You may begin your conversation with the recruiter by referring candidates, but you may end up as a potential candidate for one of the opportunities she is seeking to fill. Suppose you listen to the recruiter's description of the assignment, and a position description is forwarded for your review. You might consider referring a candidate or two, but upon reviewing the position's specs, you determine that this may be a great opportunity for you to consider. The title is the next step up for you; the compensation is very attractive; the company is one of the industry leaders; and the position is located in your hometown. Hmmm . . . let me get back in touch with the recruiter and discuss this further, you contemplate. You then call the recruiter and express your interest in the opportunity. The recruiter responds warmly if she knows you are a potential candidate. (The recruiter should also respond warmly even if you are not a viable candidate for one of her searches and should thank you graciously for your time and consideration. She should then advise you that for a specific reason or reasons your background is not suitable for a particular search but that she will be certain to keep you in mind for other assignments in the future.) The recruiter will then proceed to the next step of the qualifying stage.

Candidate Qualification Part I—The In-Depth Telephone Interview

Once the recruiter determines that your experience appears to be a potential match for an opportunity, he will conduct an in-depth telephone interview to ensure you are qualified according to skill set and how you handle yourself over the telephone. This interview may be conducted on the spot, or the recruiter will schedule a time in the next few days to complete the interview, accommodating both your and his schedule. The recruiter will ask for a copy of your resume. If your paperwork is not current, you should bring it up to date with your most recent position, responsibilities, title, and so on. (If you prove to be a viable semifinalist candidate, the recruiter will write a lengthy profile document detailing your career, but it's a good idea to keep your information current to expedite the process—again, time is of the essence!)

During the call, the recruiter may ask you to tell him a little bit about your background, and as you recount your work history, he may punctuate your narrative with questions pertinent to the qualifications he is seeking in a candidate. At my firm, the rule of thumb is to ask a candidate to walk us through her career history—and to include in this narrative the potential candidate's college education, the first job out of college, and to continue chronologically up to the present position. In this way, the candidate can provide us with more of a three-dimensional view of her background, adding in life experiences as well as work history, and we gain much broader knowledge about a candidate than we may have been able to obtain by simply asking direct questions. We may also probe for more detail once we determine whether or not the candidate is a strong potential contender.

The recruiter will want to know specific dates of employment for each job; how you secured each position (Were you recruited? Or were you promoted? Did you see an ad in a newspaper?); why you left each position (Did you leave for a better position? Were you promoted within your company? Were you laid off?); what your accomplishments as well as responsibilities were (it's one thing to cite your responsibilities and another to demonstrate how you fulfilled them), including facts and figures as to how you brought the department and company closer toward achieving its goals; details about staff supervision, whether direct reports or cross-functional team management; details about budget development and management; to whom you reported; and a description of each company—even though your company may be a household name and well-known corporate entity, describe the business, its annual revenues, and number of employees and include the location (city and state) of your office. In addition, the recruiter will want to know the components of your current compensation—base salary, bonus eligibility, stock options, and other benefits and perquisites.

You may question why the recruiter needs this information and not want to disclose it, fearing that he may limit you to searches within a specific compensation range. In fact, we recruiters strive to secure your next best career step for you—even though we represent and are paid by the client. Remember that it is in our best interest to make both the candidate and the client happy. We're in the business of building relationships and creating success stories for both parties. By providing us with your compensation information, we will be better prepared to identify opportunities that best suit your needs and your career path.

As part of this exchange process, the recruiter will share with you information about the opportunity and give you time to ask questions. You may have a full list, but the recruiter might not wish to spend an inordinate amount of time answering them for you because he may not want to give you too much information on the position or company, thus enabling you to shape your qualifications to suit the role, and the recruiter just doesn't have the luxury of time to give you at this stage of the qualifying process. Following this exchange, the recruiter may or may not determine that you are a potential candidate for an opportunity. If so, the recruiter will invite you for an in-person interview with him and will send you materials on the company or refer you to its Web site for more information prior to your meeting. If the recruiter does not believe you are a viable candidate, the individual may thank you for your time and advise you that he will see how the semifinalist panel shapes up in the coming weeks and will be in touch.

Candidate Qualification Part II—The In-Person Interview

You have now been invited for an in-person interview with the headhunter. This is a very good sign in your candidacy and viability to compete for a position that may be a terrific career move! At this point in the process, you may only be one of six or eight candidates to reach this stage of the search. That's quite a difference from where the recruiter began with possibly five hundred contacts on the list! So if you are so special, why do you need to go through an in-person meeting when the recruiter has already spent so much time on the phone with you and you feel you have been appropriately and thoroughly qualified by her? For most executive positions, you need to have not only the technical skills but also a set of *intangible* skills. These include professional demeanor, personal mind-set (do you see the glass half full or half empty), the ability to make judgment calls, the appropriate level of risk tolerance, visionary and leadership capabilities, and other such core competencies that recruiters seek in candidates who make it to the semifinalist panel. (I've devoted an entire chapter to the intangible qualities, as I believe it is critical to possess these traits in order to be successful—and I want you to be able to recognize and leverage them in your own career navigation.) Although some recruiters may believe these qualities can be assessed on the phone—or perhaps in a video interview—it is my strong opinion that to fully qualify a mid- or senior-level management candidate, the recruiter must complete an in-person interview.

During this meeting, the recruiter may ask you more pointed questions that relate to the position, including questions that gauge your intangible attributes. She may inquire as to how you may have addressed a crisis in the company, what hurdles you may have overcome to accomplish department or corporate goals, how you define your management style, and how you counseled senior management or your subordinates during a particularly challenging period. Answer these questions in a forthright manner and elaborate appropriately to drive home your strengths as a manager. This meeting will also provide you with more time to ask the recruiter about the opportunity and the company. The recruiter should be able to give you insight into the corporate culture, the temperament and personality of the individuals in the company with whom your position will interface, company financials, the career path of the position, and so on. The recruiter will expect you to have thoughtful questions, which is a good strategy and shows your interest in the opportunity. If you find your questions have been answered during the interview process, tell this to the recruiter rather than stating you have none.

Allow the recruiter to close the interview and be certain to pick up on her cues as to the conclusion of this meeting. You don't want to rush to determine the end of the interview yourself, either by closing it too early or dragging it out. You don't want to undersell or oversell yourself. If you have additional questions for the recruiter, follow up with a telephone call.

One more point worth mentioning in this process is how it is determined when and where to meet the recruiter for the in-person interview. This depends upon a number of factors, including the city in which you and the recruiter live and work and what schedules will permit. A recruiter needs to be mindful of costs as the client reimburses the search firm for all out-of-pocket expenses incurred on the client's behalf. (As I discussed in Chapter 2, these expenses are typically charged back dollar for dollar, although some firms charge a flat percentage fee instead.) I mention this because a recruiter may visit a city where he can meet several candidates for one or more searches, thus spreading the cost of the trip among clients and reducing the expense as well as travel time. The recruiter may ask you to meet him in the location where he will be meeting a number of candidates. Or you may be asked to travel to the firm's office. Your expenses for your trip will be reimbursed by the search firm.

The Next Steps Following an Interview with the Recruiter—Determining the Semifinalist Panel

The goal of the recruiter at the apex of the search cycle is to present to the hiring executives a semifinalist panel of qualified candidates. Each of the semifinalists will have been fully qualified by the recruiter in the steps I just described, and some may be internal candidates within the client company.

It will be up to the recruiter to decide who makes it to the panel. How is this decided? There are so many variables in this decision-making process. So much depends upon the timing of the search—coordinating the small space in time in which the candidate is ready to move forward with another opportunity and the time the position needs to be filled; the cultural fit between the candidate and the company; overcoming obstacles that might keep qualified candidates from accepting the opportunity, such as a trailing spouse who chooses not to relocate to the city where the job is located or overwhelming housing costs; and other such situations. There are so many reasons a recruiter may choose one candidate over another to be part of the semifinalist panel. And the decision-making process can be very difficult if he has more candidates that are either very qualified or underqualified for the opportunity. The goal of the recruiter is to present a balanced panel of qualified candidates with diverse experiences and attributes. If the sun, the moon, and all the planets align and you become a semifinalist candidate, what happens next?

Typically, a retained recruiter will develop a comprehensive candidate profile to present to the client executives. This document will include key material from your resume combined with the information that the recruiter garnered from both the in-depth telephone and in-person interviews with you. In order to expedite the process and communicate your qualifications accurately to the recruiter, it is critical for you to have a well-written resume. I'll discuss the information to include in a resume and the preferred format in the chapters that follow, but the point I want to make for purposes of this discussion is that you should be as thorough as possible in your paperwork so that your chances of a polished written presentation for the client increase exponentially. Once you are presented on paper to the client and the recruiter thoroughly reviews each semifinalist's background with the hiring authority, they will make a decision as to whom they wish to interview. The recruiter will present each candidate in the best light possible while being mindful of which candidate or candidates best exemplify the requirements of the position.

Although the recruiter will not ultimately make the decision for the client, he will help shape the decision-making process as to whom they will meet by providing a verbal comparison of the candidate's strengths and weaknesses. This brings us to the next phase of the search.

Interviews with the Client Hiring Entity

At this point, the recruiter will take the news to the semi-finalist candidates whom the client has decided to interview. This is always a delicate part of search, as it involves moving some candidates forward in the process and ruling out others who were also strong candidates. It is critical for the recruiter to maintain his relationships with the valued candidates. Equally critical, as a reputable search professional, the recruiter must rule out candidates while assuring them that although this particular opportunity will not be an option for them, the recruiter believes they are strong candidates and wishes to remain in contact with them for future assignments. Semifinalists who are invited to interview with the client should be thoroughly prepared by the recruiter prior to these meetings. This preparation may include providing up-to-the-minute information on what's happening at the company, both operationally and organizationally, and providing biographical information on each executive the candidate will meet. In today's confusing world of what to wear to an interview—T-shirt and jeans or business suit—the recruiter also may provide counsel on appropriate attire. The search firm or the client human resource contact will typically make all travel arrangements for the candidate.

The interview process with the hiring executives varies widely from client to client, both in the number and level of executives involved in the process as well as the interview style. The recruiter usually discusses the search committee chosen to interview the semifinalist candidate and recommends those who should be included in the first, second, and third round of meetings. Following these meetings, it is crucial for the candidate to connect with the recruiter and debrief from the interviews. This debriefing session gives the candidate an opportunity to review her points made during the interview and what the client executives asked her in these meetings. The recruiter also will do the same with the client executives. Following these debriefings and feedback discussions, decisions will be made as to who the two semifinalists or perhaps even the finalist candidate will be. If the client is not pleased with any of the candidates—which does happen on occasion— the recruiter will discuss with the client issues he had with each candidate, and if the search professional believes they can be overcome, he will counsel both the candidate and the client as to how this may happen. Often a candidate may be ruled out because of interviewing style. This can be difficult for a client to overcome, as he can't see beyond a gaffe made by the candidate in this critical meeting. But, come on, few people can interview flawlessly. An interview is nearly always an excruciatingly nerve-wracking experience for most individuals—even the most adept public speakers. So we head-hunters do our best to point this out to the unforgiving client.

Following these rounds of interviews, the candidate should send thank-you notes to each individual she met and provide any follow-up information or materials that the client executives requested. A rule of thumb: Always err on the more formal side in the interview process. Yes, thank-you notes are still mandated, and no, an e-mail is *not* acceptable even in today's Internet-crazed world!

Formal Referencing/Offer/Compensation Negotiations

As you will note in Figure 5.1, once a finalist is selected from among the panel, the recruiter will initiate formal referencing. Usually the recruiter will conduct the rerfence-checking portion of the process, but sometimes the in-house corporate recruiter or human resource representative at the client company may choose to perform this step. I discussed reference checking briefly in Chapter 1 and will provide you with further guidance in Chapter 11. In general, the recruiter will advise you that you have been identified as the finalist candidate (or possibly one of two finalists) and that the next step is to check references. Keep in mind that the recruiter may have already conducted informal reference checks or "stealth references" on your background prior to this point in the process. This time around, the headhunter will ask you for your references, which should include five or six individuals with whom you have interfaced in your professional life. References may include one or more former supervisors, peers, subordinates, and perhaps outside professional contacts or vendors who may be able to assess your abilities.

Once the recruiter has received positive comments from your references and turned them over to the client (and hopefully they will be a positive reflection on your candidacy), a decision on an offer will be made. Sometimes an offer will be presented prior to completion of the reference-checking step—particularly if the client requires an extensive background or drug test performed by outside vendors—but the offer will be contingent upon satisfactory results of all those procedures. Who makes the offer to you? That varies from client to client as well. It is in your best interest for the recruiter to make the offer, as it enables you to voice your concerns with the components and takes the onus off you to negotiate with your future boss. Again, although the recruiter is paid by and represents the client, it is in everyone's best interest for you to receive an attractive offer, and the recruiter should take any concerns you may have about the offer to the client and work on a satisfactory agreement for both parties. Final acceptance of the offer can either be made to the recruiter, who will then share the good news with the client, or depending upon circumstances, you may wish to accept the offer directly with the hiring executive.

I will provide you with more detail on all of these steps in the search process, including what to expect in an offer, how much time you have to respond to an offer, giving notice at your current position, and other such points in subsequent chapters.

At Last, the Search Is Completed!

Following your acceptance of the offer and an agreed-upon start date, the recruiter will advise all candidates, sources, and others involved in the search process of the identity of the successful candidate and thank them for their participation. Our firm typically communicates this by sending a letter to all of those individuals whom we contacted. Included in this letter are not only words of appreciation for their assistance but also a brief biography on the successful candidate who accepted the position. This final step closes the loop with all involved during what typically takes 90 to 120 days to complete and further builds the relationship with these individuals. And that's a critical part of executive search!

So I've covered the basic mechanics of the search process—the nuts and bolts, if you will, of how a typical retained search progresses and how the candidate is moved forward throughout the adventure commonly known as executive search. Now you should be better prepared for what to anticipate during the process and better appreciate the time it takes to complete a search. Ultimately, having knowledge of all the steps involved in identifying qualified candidates for executive-level opportunities will improve your chances of successful career navigation.

Secret: The whole is greater than the sum of its parts. Focus on building a complete relationship with a headhunter. Don't just settle for the thrill of a momentary "transaction high."

CHAPTER 6

The Importance of Etiquette in Your Relationship with a Recruiter

Secrets to the Softer Side of Search

Having reviewed my search secrets up to this point, you may feel confident that you better understand the mechanics involved in working with a recruiter—the nuts and bolts of the search process. You now have a good sense of what to expect when a recruiter contacts you as a potential candidate and a general knowledge of the steps that may take you toward securing a new opportunity. You also have an idea of when it's appropriate to contact the recruiter, when you may anticipate a call from him or her, and how and when the recruiter will move you forward in the search process. And you've gained an insight into what's involved in being a recruiter's source—

a contact that may serve as a referral of candidates to the search professional.

But there's more to executive search than the hard-wired fundamentals of the relationship. Headhunting is a human capital endeavor. We're not in the business of making widgets. There's a much softer, human side to this profession. It's a people business, and when dealing with people, there must be a set of working guidelines to follow in terms of etiquette. Now, when I say *etiquette*, I'm not speaking of table manners; I'm talking about common courtesies that are practiced in the corporate world. Although knowing and following business etiquette may seem like common sense to many of you in the work environment, the lines can become fuzzy when one is not entirely sure what role the recruiter represents to the candidate. There are those who may misinterpret a recruiter's intermediary function between candidate and client as that of psychotherapist, mother/father, best friend, soothsayer, or tea leaf reader. In other words, some professionals may think the role a recruiter plays may allow the candidate license to "let it all hang out," if I may borrow a phrase from the 1960s counterculture.

Allow me to set the record straight. Rule number one when interacting with a search professional on any level is this: Remember that our role is to assess your qualifications as a candidate for searches we are conducting on behalf of our clients. Everything you say and do impacts our decision as to whether or not to move you forward in the process. Take your cues from Journalism 101—nothing you say to a reporter is off the record. The same principle applies to your dealings with headhunters. We are seeing, feeling, and judging human beings, and it's our role to lessen the risk of placing you in a job with one of our client companies. Having an overall understanding and implementation of this general rule is critical in the working relationship between the candidate and the recruiter. Otherwise, reaching the ultimate end goal of completing a search with a happy client, happy candidate, and happy recruiter is impossible to attain.

Let me give you an example of how your behavior may impact your candidacy in a search. Suppose you send your resume to an executive search firm in hopes of securing an interview. A recruiter reviews the document and believes you might be a viable candidate for one of her searches. The search professional calls you and initiates a dialogue about her interest in learning more about your background—that your resume has piqued her interest and the recruiter would like to get to know you better. You are delighted that this individual has contacted you. However, the recruiter is immediately put off by the fact that your conversation is punctuated by the loud cracking of chewing gum and thinks, hmmm . . . if this person talks to me while chomping on a big wad of gum, would the candidate do the same in an interview with the client? The recruiter decides to end the call and move on to the next resume, dials a number and connects with another potential candidate—you. The phone interview goes very well, and the recruiter is relieved that you are a very articulate, highly professional, and polite person. (No gum chewing, no tobacco chewing, no chewing of any kind goes on during the conversation.) The recruiter decides to invite you for an in-person interview. Feeling confident that this interview will go equally as well as the phone screen, you become fairly comfortable with the recruiter, sit down opposite her, swing your legs over the side of the chair, and begin to tell your life story. Unfortunately the recruiter has stopped listening, unable to get beyond your inappropriate conduct.

Although these activities might appear to be only mildly offensive, the search professional sees your actions as not only poor manners but also poor judgment on your part to behave so casually during an interview that could lead to your next best career step. But wait a minute, you think. I'm not interviewing with the hiring executive. How I behave with the recruiter shouldn't matter. It's just the recruiter! As the conduit of information to the client executives about how a candidate comports himself, I'll let you in on a little secret—you better believe your behavior with the recruiter matters!

You may already know your business etiquette. However, not everyone recognizes that certain behavior can be construed as potentially offensive under certain circumstances such as when you are dealing with a recruiter! No one is expected to be perfect; there is no such thing as perfect as it is all subjective. However, I'd like to provide you with certain guidelines to follow to ensure you do not commit any gaffes that the executive search community frowns upon. My "Top 30 Do's and Don'ts of Headhunter Etiquette" represent some of the most ridiculous, unprofessional, and inane things that you *shouldn't* do in your relationship with a recruiter. Are you ready? Here we go!

Don't Bare Your Soul

When you meet with a recruiter, you are expected to disclose certain information about your professional background to enable him to accurately present you as a viable candidate. That is a typical part of the interview process. But what should you disclose about your personal background? Although there are laws that protect your privacy and ensure that a prospective employer does not discriminate against you based on ethnic background, religious beliefs, age, and so on, there are no laws preventing you from voluntarily sharing your innermost secrets to the recruiter. However, there are guidelines you should follow in presenting content beyond career facts. After all, is it appropriate for you to let the recruiter know how much you hate your mother-in-law? Remember that you are sitting down with a recruiter, not a psychotherapist. In short, don't share your innermost secrets because they probably don't relate to the job. Indeed, one of the difficult decisions you must make when navigating your career is deciding how much information to share with a recruiter. In this instance, one of the old-fashioned adages is still the most applicable today: Honesty is the best policy. Be candid, direct, honest, and professional in your dealings with the executive search community, and this will result in the most effective and productive relationship for both you and the recruiter.

Don't Expect the Recruiter to Be Your Best Friend

Just because the recruiter is friendly with you doesn't mean he wants you to be his best friend. This is a business. Again, there's a fine line in terms of how to put into perspective this type of relationship. After all, you walk down some very emotional paths with the recruiter. A job change is one of the most significant changes an individual can experience in a lifetime. Changing jobs is as stressful as weddings, childbirth, funerals, graduations, and first-time home buying. Those who are involved in these milestones of life are your loved ones. Similarly, the headhunter will share in your joy of becoming a successful candidate in one of his searches. It's a meaningful moment for the recruiter as well. It can become particularly emotional when there have been hurdles to overcome during the process. There are also strong feelings involved when the candidate is ruled out of the search. Clearly, there are many bonding moments between recruiter and candidate, and friendships can develop. And the longer you know the executive search professional, the more familiar the relationship becomes.

Please be cautious about letting your emotions get to you during the search process. The recruiter certainly can be your counselor, your sounding board, and your career navigator—but don't let your emotions run amok! Doing so can be especially perilous for you under certain circumstances. Suppose you know about a search that the recruiter is conducting and you are very interested in the opportunity. For whatever reason, she doesn't contact you. Your feelings are hurt. After all, we're friends, you think. How could she not call me? Well, the recruiter did not believe you were qualified for this particular opportunity. Remember, the profession I am in is not all about placing friends in great jobs—it's about bringing candidates their next best career step and bringing corporations superior talent.

So when you interview for a position, when and how do you set the professional friendship aside? It is all about how to be appropriate in the relationship. Again, business etiquette remains the rule of the day.

Don't Use Demeaning Forms of Address with the Recruiter

In an effort to become comfortable with executive search professionals, you may attempt to expedite the process by using overly familiar terms of address with them. Not a good idea. In addressing recruiters—or anyone but your close friends or loved ones for that matter—it's always best to use more formal salutations. You don't have to go so far as to use Mr., Ms., or Mrs., but don't approach a recruiter and say, "Hey, buddy" or "There's my gal" or even "How are you, sweetie?" As a rule, steer clear of using these familiar forms of address, as well as calling adult women girls or gals or grown men boys, guys, or buddies. Not all of these words are forbidden in your conversation with a recruiter, but until you gauge the basis of your relationship with him and the tolerance level for what could be construed as a lack of professionalism in your conversation (remember, the recruiter is listening and watching for any inappropriate language or behavior that you may employ in speaking with his client!), please err on the more formal side in your conversations and overall behavior.

Don't Manipulate Your Background and Experience to Fit the Opportunity

Our job as recruiters is to find the candidate most suited to the position we are seeking to fill on behalf of our clients. You have figured this out. It's simple. How do you get a job through a recruiter? Just write your resume to fit a specific job description and you've duped the recruiter into believing you are qualified for the job. Wrong! A recruiter interviews hundreds of candidates a year and can easily recognize when a candidate is, let's say (to be kind), stretching the truth about his background and experience. How? By conducting an in-depth interview with you and exploring all of your accomplishments—not just focusing on your responsibilities in your prior roles. A search professional wants to know what you accomplished in each of your positions, complete with verifiable facts and figures. Similar to the book and film by the same name, *Six Degrees of Separation,* you can usually make a connection between two people on earth through six people or less that each of them knows. (This concept was based on the principle developed by the Nobel Prize–winning inventor of the telegraph, Guglielmo Marconi.) It's a much narrower separation in the search community. We conduct stealth referencing on candidates to verify what they are telling us is true. Someone we know will know someone who knows you. A few phone calls and any truth stretching will be exposed—and you as a potential candidate will be crossed off our list of contacts forever. You may think that a little white lie here or there can't hurt. Maybe you oversaw a staff of 10 instead of 15. Or you reported to the vice president instead of the CEO. What's the difference? The difference is between a candidate who is honest and forthright and uses good judgment in portraying his or her qualifications and one who feels the need to elaborate beyond the bounds of truth to feel qualified for a job. You end up reeking of desperation, and the search community will sniff you out promptly.

Don't Be Arrogant or Pretentious

You may be a descendant of one of the wealthiest families in the world. You may have degrees from all the right prep schools and Ivy League colleges and have membership in all the right clubs. Does this make you a better candidate than someone who was born into a family of more modest means and graduated from state schools? Someone whose first job was working as a waitress to put herself through college?

Hardly. On the contrary, recruiters want to see a candidate who is a self-starter—who has taken the initiative in life and has been successful in her own right. Do we frown on candidates who have all the pedigrees? No. However, the crux of our qualification process is to learn what candidates have accomplished *themselves* in their career. We don't care about tales from the frat house at Harvard or your debutante ball or your direct blood ties to the Astors, the Rockefellers, the Buffets, or the Gateses. Save the stories about your descendants who arrived on the *Mayflower* for your grandchildren. What purpose does this information serve in our attempt to qualify you for an opportunity? Focus exclusively on topics that are germane to the job.

Similarly, telling the recruiter that you have all the money in the world and you really don't need to work is not going to support your candidacy any more than someone who tells us how much they really need the job to pay all their overdue bills. So even if your pedigree is one that would make a blue-ribbon heifer at the state fair envious, what matters to recruiters is your successful career track and how well you might perform in the next role we very well may bring you.

Neither do we want you to be boastful about how successful you have been in your career. It's one thing to be proud of your accomplishments and share this information with us with emphasis but another to be arrogant in your presentation. A braggart can translate into a poor team player or leader.

Don't Discuss How Much Money the Recruiter Will Make If He or She Places You in the Position

We all know what headhunters do for a living, but retained recruiters are not body brokers. As I discussed in prior chapters, retained recruiters receive payment from clients whether they place a candidate or not. This is because they perform a broad array of professional services and not just candidate identification. Just as in any consulting role, retained recruiters receive payment for the service they provide. Calling recruiters and saying it's their lucky day because you are a great candidate and by placing you in a job, they'll be making a pile of money is hardly a sound approach to use in working with the search community. Even if you are highly qualified on paper for an opportunity, calling and making this type of statement demonstrates poor judgment on your part and really gets under the skin of the recruiter!

Don't Expect an Interview to Translate into a Job Offer

Some individuals believe that just because they have been invited to meet with a recruiter, the interview will automatically translate into a job offer. You may be one of dozens of potential candidates or sources whom a recruiter may contact during the life of a search. Don't be offended. Contacting several professionals for an assignment is critical to ensure that the recruiter finds the best-suited candidate for the opportunity he is seeking to fill. You may end up being moved forward in the process by the recruiter—or you may be a source of candidates for the recruiter. Either way, don't consider the contact with the search professional a waste of time if your interview does not result in a meeting with the client executives or an offer. Make every interaction with the recruiter a positive and productive experience, and over time, you might be placed in a position through this individual.

Another note: When you receive an offer from a company during the interview, it's best to hold off on negotiating at the time of the offer. Take a day or two to come back with your wish list. You don't want to jeopardize the offer, but you also don't want to be hasty in your decision-making process. It's best to thank the interviewer for the offer and then immediately contact the recruiter to guide you through the negotiating process.

Don't Accept an Interview with a Company Unless You Are Genuinely Interested

Perhaps you have spoken with a number of recruiters about opportunities, and none of them have appealed to you. You might think that the recruiters will stop calling you if you don't play the game and accept one of their overtures to meet with a client. Not true. We don't expect you to be interested in every opportunity we present to you. Although we may become familiar with your requirements to make a job change, we can't fully anticipate specifically what will pique your interest and what won't. However, if after being fully qualified by the recruiter you decide to interview with the client, move forward in earnest, not just to pacify the search professional. And, never, never accept an interview as a way to get a free trip to the city where your folks live or where the temperature is kinder than where you live. Taking advantage of the interview situation in this manner will end up costing the client company time and money and will reflect poorly on your potential candidacy in future opportunities you may have an interest in pursuing with the recruiter. If the recruiter sees this type of behavior in a candidate, it's grounds for deleting your name from the firm's database as, again, it shows you are exercising poor judgment. And for you as a potential candidate, let's say that after meeting you, the hiring authority wants to make you an offer. You'll just wind up having to concoct some inane excuse as to why you can't accept the post. In short, you'll look foolish all the way around.

Don't Ramble On When Interviewing

In the interview with the recruiter, you launch yourself into an hour-and-a-half monologue when asked to give a brief synopsis of your background. A professional recruiter can sum up your candidacy in the first few minutes of the meeting.

There's no need to monopolize the conversation and risk losing the attention of the interviewer. Focus on the highlights of your career and your accomplishments. Be sure to let the recruiter ask questions throughout. If he wants you to elaborate on a certain point, the interviewer will ask. Don't shut him out of the conversation by talking over him. The search professional wants to learn about your background, but it serves no purpose for you to prove how assertive you are by showing who is in charge of the interview. Quite the contrary. Be concise. Give a 5- to 10-minute overview of your experience and punctuate it with key points and accomplishments that are relevant to the position you are pursuing. If you've held positions that are not exact matches to the opportunity, think of ways your accomplishments in these roles showcase your intangible attributes, such as good judgment or leadership skills. A recruiter wants to hear you hit the high points of your career to date and how it relates to the assignment, not deliver a casual stroll down memory lane.

Don't Demean or Badmouth Your Prior Employers

We've all heard our coworkers vent about the boss, colleagues, subordinates, or annoying situations at the office. Every office environment has its irritants. Certainly appropriate venting has its place. Family members come in handy for that, but not headhunters. Sour grapes never taste good to recruiters. Demeaning or badmouthing your prior employers shows bad judgment. It also raises questions as to who might be telling the truth. Perhaps the candidate was a difficult employee. It's always a two-sided equation. Although you want to be accurate in characterizing the environment in which you worked, use caution in presenting negative information about current or previous employers. If you work for a well-known company, its culture and management are likely to be known by the recruiter. Use diplomacy in your depiction of a bad situation.

Also stay away from gossiping about people with whom you currently or previously worked. Spending too much time at the water cooler would disqualify most candidates from participation in a search.

Don't Be Late

Be punctual. Nothing sends a worse signal from a candidate who is late to an interview with a recruiter or potential employer. It shows lack of respect and sends a message that the candidate is disorganized, scattered, and displays poor planning skills. Although some instances make being late unavoidable—such as weather delays or other cancellations at the airport, traffic jams, or a last-minute meeting called by the CEO—do your best to schedule appointments during periods where time constraints may not be as tight. Perhaps your best time is early morning on a Friday when the pace may be less hectic at the office, or in the evenings. And always exchange contact information with the recruiter—preferably your cell phone number or some other way to contact you should the recruiter be running late due to unavoidable circumstances. We all try to be as flexible as possible, but please do your best to be on time for interviews.

Don't Interview when Ill

Some candidates fear losing out on an opportunity by canceling an appointment with a recruiter due to illness. Trust me. I'll forgive you for rescheduling your meeting if you are ill. You never interview as well when you feel poorly, and you risk sharing your bug with the recruiter and other members of the search firm. Coughing and sneezing during an interview is poor form. And would you really want to shake someone's hand after it has shielded a hearty sneeze?

Don't Throw Any Tantrums

Don't be a sore loser if you are not the candidate selected for the job. Be professional and be open minded about learning what you should perhaps do differently the next time. Just because you were not made an offer for this one particular opportunity doesn't mean you are a bad candidate—after all, you may have been selected from among hundreds of candidates and progressed to the semifinalist panel. You should feel pride in getting that far in the search process. We'll contact you for future opportunities unless you throw a fit and scream at the recruiter. No one wants to recruit a short-tempered bully.

Don't Complain about the Search Process

The search process can take 90 to 120 days to complete for most executive-level opportunities. Sometimes the time frame is shorter; sometimes, longer. Although I have placed candidates within a three-week window, it is highly unlikely that the search will complete that quickly. Once you reach the point in your career where you are likely to be placed in your next position by a recruiter, the process typically involves multiple interviews with the executive search firm and the potential hiring executives. Scheduling these interviews can be an arduous task. You are a busy executive, and so are the client contacts. Physical distance among these individuals complicates the situation. It's fine to express concern if you feel the recruiter has been unresponsive, but please be patient with the process overall. Again, we're not in the widget-making business. We're dealing with human beings.

Don't Let Your Ego Get out of Control

I always say, check your ego at the door when interviewing, when you accept a new position, and throughout your overall career navigation. An unselfish work style is mandated to be successful in most positions and most corporate cultures. Healthy confidence is respected and shows strong leadership abilities, but an arrogant disposition and overbearing ego won't wear well on the search community.

Don't Wear Strong Perfumes or Colognes

Avoid wearing strong perfumes or colognes when interviewing with the recruiter or the client company. There's the tried-and-true saying that you want someone to remember you, not your perfume. In a business setting, fragrance can be not only distracting but also offensive. Some people are highly allergic to fragrance. In fact, some offices, restaurants, hospitals, and other public areas are fragrance free, just as smoking has become banned in these locales. Similar to shaking someone's hand following a sneezing fit, you don't want to shake someone's hand and have his fragrance linger for hours. One of my recruiters interviewed a potential candidate whose perfume was so strong that the administrative staff had to open the doors to admit fresh air. It was overwhelming and distracted the recruiter from focusing on the candidate's accomplishments. The odor lingered for hours. And when a member of our finance department received the candidate's travel expense receipts, she said the paperwork was steeped in her perfume. Strong fragrance should be reserved for personal, not business, use. What message are you trying to convey by wearing such a strong scent, anyway?

Don't Send a Photo of Yourself with Your Resume

Your resume should tell your professional history without photos of yourself. It's highly inappropriate to accompany your resume with a photo for an executive-level position. Professional demeanor and presentation style are important qualities to possess, but would you feel comfortable knowing a recruiter called you only because he liked your picture? Are you seeking a date or a job? Although that may seem a harsh judgment for your good intentions, your qualifications and accomplishments should stand on their own merit without a photo essay. If appearance is a key part of someone's job—such as an actor, fashion model, or possibly TV newscaster—it's an expected part of your curriculum vitae. Otherwise, lose the photo.

Don't Send In the Buffaloes

Sending gifts or other trinkets with your resume will not increase your chances of becoming a candidate in a search. In fact, those items can be annoying to deal with. And some firms don't accept any gifts over a certain amount or of a certain kind as they can smack of bribery or set up the wrong expectations. Don't send gift baskets, boxes of candy or cookies, or stuffed animals along with your paperwork. I remember the time when a young professional wanted to clearly set herself apart from the multitudes of resumes received by our firm. However, her need to send a stuffed toy buffalo along with her resume as a means of distinguishing herself demonstrated immaturity and lack of judgment. Just because she wanted to stand out and make a point that she hailed from Montana didn't mean she could add value to a client organization.

Similarly, don't send the search firm a huge packet of samples—case histories, videos, or other lengthy documents. The recruiter does not have time to review them all, and storage becomes a problem. Further, we do not want responsibility for original samples. Based on Murphy's Law, between potential shipping and storage problems, irreplaceable materials will inevitably get lost! So please, no gimmicks or bulky samples.

Don't Harass or Hound the Recruiter

Appropriate persistence is one thing, but calling and badgering the recruiter is another. We understand it can be frustrating when a recruiter is not responsive to your overtures. When you send a resume to a search firm to be included on the list of potential candidates, you expect to receive a response. But you don't hear from them. You then call and insist on speaking to someone, or you send a barrage of e-mail messages or follow-up notes. Why don't recruiters return your attempts to contact them? There are several reasons. One could be that your behavior is so overly aggressive that the recruiter views you as lacking in good judgment and does not want to include you in his database of contacts. Two, your background may not be suited for the type of searches the firm conducts, and your resume is among hundreds like this. To respond to every resume by phone or mail, the firm would need to hire either a direct-mail service or administrative assistant for this purpose, and the cost of such an endeavor would be prohibitive. And three, with headhunters working on several searches at once and interfacing with hundreds of potential candidates, they may take a few days to a couple of weeks to connect with you. His intentions are good, but there are just too few hours in a day to be able to contact everyone who calls, particularly if you are not active in a search. I follow the rule that if I cannot connect with an individual promptly, I will do my best to schedule a time in the future to talk, and my assistant will be in touch. Most importantly, trust that we are operating in everyone's best interests and that we will respond to you appropriately and in due time.

Don't Call and Only Say, "Hi, It's John"

Nothing can be more frustrating for a recruiter than to receive a call or phone message from someone whom only gives a first name. Calling and saying, "Hi, it's John returning your call," leads only to a potentially embarrassing moment for both recruiter and candidate. Even if the recruiter has just called you, she may be in the process of contacting several individuals with the first name of John or Steve or Mary or Sue—all within one hour! If you call and identify yourself only by your first name, the recruiter then needs to ask your last name. You may feel put off and say, "You just called me," inferring that the recruiter must be so stupid as to not remember you and why she was calling. Remember, recruiters are typically working on several searches at a time and may make a hundred phone calls in a day. Yes, they will usually remember you, but unless you are a spouse or a child of the recruiter, please err on the more formal side. Identify yourself by your full name and remind the recruiter why she was calling you. Again, the recruiter may have just left messages for four potential candidates for one of many searches, and they all might be named John. We appreciate your compliance with this courtesy.

Don't Write a Nasty Note to the Recruiter If You Don't Get the Job

"Sour grapes" takes on a whole new meaning in this context. Although you may feel hurt and extremely disappointed that you were not selected as the successful candidate in a search, you will not score points with the recruiter by writing an angry note to him after being ruled out. Oftentimes candidates who are moved forward in a search will psychologically place themselves in the job for which they are interviewing. Before making it to the second round, some candidates will already have picked out their new house, have decorated their office at the new company, and have planned a big celebration when the moment of offer comes. When the offer doesn't come, they are deflated at hot-air-balloon proportions. It isn't fair to yourself to put yourself in a job before you receive an offer and then take it out on the recruiter for not making it happen for you. Be realistic, use good judgment, and be professional!

Don't Abuse the Receptionist

It may seem an obvious breach of business etiquette to call and yell at the receptionist at the search firm, but for some reason this level of poor judgment remains an affliction for many hopeful candidates. Don't they realize that the receptionist is a valued part of the administrative staff and doesn't deserve such abuse just because the recruiter hasn't returned a call or the individual didn't get an interview? And don't they realize that the receptionist will report such conduct to the very recruiter the caller is trying to reach? That kind of rude behavior is unacceptable in the search community.

Don't Circumvent the Recruiter and Call the Potential Employer Yourself

You are assured of spoiling your chances of being contacted by a recruiter if you already have been ruled out of a search and call the hiring executive at the client company directly. After all, you think, the search professional can't possibly be smart enough to know your qualifications for the job or how great you are. What you need to understand is that the client retains a search firm to fully screen and qualify candidates for them, as they may not have the time, the human resources, or the expertise to perform this function. They rely on the judgment of the recruiter, and the client also trusts the recruiter's judgment. If you circumvent the recruiter and contact the client yourself, the company will bounce your resume right back to the retained recruiter who advised you that you would not be a candidate in the search. This situation will serve only to embarrass you and take you off the recruiter's list of candidates to contact for future opportunities.

Do Make Yourself Available

A recruiter wants a responsive candidate. As a search progresses and the recruiter chooses to present you to the client executives, he wants you to be receptive to a meeting time or place. If you are truly interested in an opportunity, do your best to make yourself available for the meetings. Remember, time is of the essence. Hiring executives need to fill critical positions. If you use Aunt Sally's latest face-lift surgery as a reason to not be available for an interview, the recruiter may move to the next candidate on the semifinalist panel and will question your true interest in the opportunity.

Do Give the Recruiter Your Compensation Information

Recruiters need to know your compensation information or salary history. It is an important part of the search process, as the recruiter needs to know a baseline for an appropriate compensation target. Although you may fear speaking first and forever being bound to a certain range, get over it. That's not the recruiter's purpose in learning this information. We need to know your compensation for a number of reasons, but one that's key to progressing in your career is for us to negotiate on your behalf when the offer comes your way. Otherwise, when the client checks into your salary history and discovers you are so far out of the range and questions why your compensation is either so high or so low, we will not be able to go to bat for you. And when you provide us with this information, please break out your figures separately to include base salary, target annual bonus, stock options, and so on rather than a lump sum of "the high six figures." By the way, most employers ask for compensation verification—so be accurate and truthful.

Don't Assume Business Casual Is Okay for an Interview

Don't save your Sunday best just for meetings with the hiring entity's executives. Be in your best form with us as well. Don't wear jeans just because it's Friday or shorts and a T-shirt because you work for a technology company. You should not assume that because you are meeting with the recruiter and not the potential employer that you shouldn't present yourself in a professional manner. The headhunter wants to know how you might interview with the client executives, and that includes proper manner of dress. In today's corporate world that can be confusing, so you should feel comfortable discussing appropriate attire with the recruiter. You might mention to the recruiter that you will be meeting her during the work day and you will be dressed in khakis and a sports shirt or a casual dress—is that okay? The recruiter will quickly see that you understand the importance of professional demeanor with the search professional and have shown proper respect for her opinion in this area.

Don't Think You're a Candidate for Every Job

We have a handful of candidates who call us and send us their resume for *every search we conduct.* These professionals somehow believe they are perfect for every position they know we are handling. They need a reality check! They cannot possibly have every qualification for each assignment we have. It shows poor judgment and desperation to believe you should be a candidate for every posting. Be selective in the opportunity you target and for which you contact the recruiter.

Don't Tell Us Your Career Has Been Perfect

When a search professional wants to get to know you, he expects that you will have experienced some bumps along the career route. I call these "career mulligans." After all, we're dealing with human capital. No one is perfect. We want to know the real you. If you accepted a position and it wasn't what you expected it to be and left the job after a few months, tell us about it. Don't leave it out thinking it will tarnish your platinum career. Be open and honest. We understand when you don't want to remain in a less-than-optimal situation. In fact, we may question why you *wouldn't* change jobs when a company is asking you to compromise your work ethic or perform unsavory acts. However, recognize that we don't want you to bare your soul, as I discussed earlier in this chapter.

Don't Forget Your Table Manners

Dining etiquette is a mainstay of business etiquette because a significant part of an executive's work is conducted over meals. In this context, your manners do matter. Oscar Wilde said, "The world was my oyster, but I used the wrong fork." Certainly if you have poor table manners during an interview, the hiring executive will take your faux pas into consideration when deciding who the successful candidate will be. I'm not here to instruct you in table manners. There are plenty of books on social and dining etiquette for you to read. In fact, there are business etiquette classes in which you may enroll, which become particularly important—indeed critical—when dealing with international contacts. Some companies offer business etiquette seminars in house. Social etiquette usually is included in these seminars. I suggest you brush up on your dining etiquette prior to an interview that involves a meal so you won't be ruled out of a search for picking up the wrong utensil!

Don't Try to Date the Search Professional or the Client Executives or Staff Members

You are invited to meet with the search professional for her to assess your qualifications as a candidate, not a potential mate. Although it's perfectly acceptable for a more personal relationship to develop over time, both parties willing, of course, your first introduction to the recruiter and the hiring executives should remain on the professional level. Don't laugh! I once had a candidate in a search who, in the lobby of the client company where he was interviewing, began insisting that the receptionist go on a date with him. Now, he did not share this information with me; the client did! You can imagine how inappropriate this behavior was under such circumstances. He showed extremely poor judgment as a candidate, and his actions had the potential to reflect badly on our firm for sending him to the company. Please keep your emotions in check when meeting with a recruiter or in the hiring executive's offices.

True to form, in spite of the fact that the rules of yesterday's jungle are gone, the old-fashioned courtesies from business long ago still apply. You should always be a good communicator, use common sense, be polite, and always err on the side of formality. Remember, it is critical for the behavioral aspects of the relationship between recruiter and candidate to remain on the professional level. Everything you say and do will convey a message to the recruiter or hiring authority.

Secret: Emily Post would quiver with delight if she recognized how much she has influenced corporate America on the subject of etiquette. Remember one thing—if you trip and fall, it's not the blunder you should worry about; rather, it's all about how gracefully you pick yourself up!

CHAPTER 7

The Intangible Qualities versus Career Track Record

How the Search Community Evaluates a Candidate Based on Two Categories

There is an ongoing debate among the search community as to the importance of intangible qualities versus career track record in evaluating a candidate. Specific skill sets are critical to a candidate's ability to perform well in his job, but the intangible qualities, in my opinion, set someone apart from the pack. Some in the search business believe that intangible qualities—or core competencies and attributes—don't amount to much in finding a top-notch candidate. However, if you believe you can find a great job and build career momentum based on your technical job skills and college degrees alone, you're dead wrong. Over the course of my tenure in executive search and human resources, I have found that it's far more important for a candidate to possess specific intangible attributes than the technical or textbook skills he brings to the table. Although this notion may seem contrary to logic or to what you've been taught over the years, the reality proves to us that the most important competencies have little to do with skills, training, or work experience.

What are the intangible attributes one must possess? How can you ensure that you will either navigate your career successfully or fail miserably, despite intelligence, education, and experience? It is essential for you to understand these core competency criteria to move your career ahead. It is also critical that you recognize them in yourself and make these qualities known to a recruiter during the interviewing process.

I have identified and trademarked a set of core competencies that hiring executives seek in candidates today. I call them The 14 Benchmark Criteria for Evaluating Candidates. My recruitment staff and I use these criteria in assessing individuals on behalf of our clients—from Fortune 500, large-cap companies to small-cap companies and start-ups. The companies we work with don't want B- and C-level players; they have higher expectations for the quality and caliber of professionals to lead their companies. All they want to see are A or A+ players. Anything less is unacceptable. Our role as executive recruiters is to minimize the hiring risk for our client companies as well as to minimize risk for the professionals who become our candidates. By using these core competencies as an assessment standard, we minimize the risk for both parties. Let me share the secrets of these 14 intangible attributes and how you may recognize them in yourself and leverage them in your career navigation.

Personal Mind-Set

Your personal mind-set is all about how you navigate your life, how you approach it. Do you view the glass as half empty or half full? Are you open minded or closed minded? Do you have a negative attitude or a positive attitude? It's how you approach a fork in the road and which path you choose to walk down that separates success from failure.

It's unfortunate that our society has evolved into a dominance of individuals who are reluctant to explore a different road. They want what's comfortable, what's easily put before them. They are linear in their approach to their lives, their jobs, and their careers. They walk through life methodically, with their only goal being to reach retirement. Instead of looking for a new direction, a new road to explore, they just walk that tired, old, beaten path.

Those who are truly successful, however, are trailblazers. They're anything but linear in their way of thinking. Successful people are comfortable with a mind-set that's open to adventure and exploration. They consider life—in their every waking minute—an adventure. In my more than a decade of running my business, I have found that this type of mind-set, this spark, is present only in about 25 percent of individuals.

A while back, one of my executive recruiters recounted a story about a positive mind-set at work. One day she was having lunch with a client, the CEO of a Fortune 500 company, and he noticed a young busboy in the restaurant vigorously cleaning a table and carefully rearranging the place settings, flowers, and condiments. How much pride the busboy had in what he was doing really showed. The client pointed him out and said, "You see that young man? I'd hire him in a second, because he has the right attitude—the right mind-set—to be a good employee. I can teach him the skills he needs, but I can't teach him to have that kind of attitude." Although I do not know if the client ever offered this young man a job, with that kind of visible enthusiasm and positive mind-set, he undoubtedly became successful in life.

Conversely, a negative mind-set lacks that can-do attitude. Someone with this mind-set is always quick to identify the hurdles and is lagging in finding the solutions. These individuals constantly put up obstacles as to why something can't be done. For example, a former colleague of mine was the epitome of a negative mind-set. Whenever she was assigned a project, instead of just moving headlong into it, she would take three or four hours to write a memo outlining all the reasons why she couldn't accomplish it. If she had had a positive, proactive mind-set, she would have had the project completed long before the time it took her to finish writing the memo!

Individuals who are hired and promoted are those with a positive mind-set. And hiring executives can safely recognize in the first 10 minutes of talking with a candidate what type of mind-set he has. If you have a positive mind-set, you are open to and embrace change; you'll step outside the boundaries, where others are trained to take the safe roads and not take risks. Having a positive mind-set allows you to be receptive beyond your current role and responsibilities, whereas the negative mind-set says, "They don't pay me enough to do that. If they start paying me more, then maybe I'll start doing more." An overachiever has a positive mind-set—he does more than the job requires. Those are the employees who get promoted.

If you have a positive mind-set, you have a much better chance of being the very best in your chosen area of expertise. You'll walk the road to success.

Enterprising Thought Process/ Imagination and Ingenuity

Putting imagination to work is vital to your career navigation, no matter your chosen industry or profession. In fact, in most cases, if you possess an imaginative, enterprising thought process, you'll feel greatly fulfilled in both your professional and personal life. No matter what the project, the problem, or the objective, you need to be enterprising to reach your goals.

What are some of the characteristics of someone who is enterprising? Typically, such people have an endless imagination and boundless energy to dedicate to the task at hand. You know the type. Someone who is enterprising will come up with 100 ideas to find the 2 that work. And she will recognize that the discarded 98 are unimportant and move forward with the 2 best ideas, leveraging her creativity to its fullest. What is most important is *reaching* the goal and the *desire* behind the attempt to reach it. Enterprising people establish goals, monitor their progress toward them, and ultimately achieve them. They are results oriented, devoting a lot of energy to reaching their goal. Simply put, it's all about approach.

For example, a few years ago I interviewed a candidate who was the head of internal communications for a Fortune 500 company and was one of the most enterprising and imaginative people I have ever met. He was well ahead of his time in that instead of approaching the internal communications responsibilities from the more traditional, historical approach of a company newsletter and a company picnic, he analyzed the entire workforce and broke it down into myriad segments—from the truck drivers to the warehouse floor to the executive suite. He then designed communications programs that were tailored to each of those internal segments. They all received the same information, the same message, yet it was through different media to which each could relate. For example, the candidate recognized that truck drivers, who don't sit all day at a computer terminal, needed to be addressed in ways that would reach them. This enterprising professional made it happen—well ahead of sophisticated internal communications programs becoming a reality in corporate America. What was his thought process? He looked at the challenge before him: How could he effectively communicate to 15,000 people? How could he do it in a timely fashion? Would employees be receptive to his program? He found the creative solutions to these challenges—ones that worked. That's an enterprising thought process. That's using ingenuity, creativity, and imagination to meet and exceed expectations. And that's the type of professional whom recruiters move forward in the search process and whom hiring executives employ.

What do recruiters look for when determining whether or not a candidate is enterprising? Two points you should remember as you travel the career path:

1. Be receptive to new ideas and recognize the importance of a fresh perspective rather than the tried and true. In other words, think out of the box, not off the shelf. Let the creative juices flow and channel them into ways that will *exceed* corporate and departmental goals; and,
2. Live that timeless adage: Work smarter, not harder.

Drive and Enthusiasm

A professional with drive and enthusiasm clearly stands out from the pack. It's evident in the way an individual approaches any task he chooses to undertake. Over the years, I have interviewed countless individuals who are lacking in drive. Somehow they have managed to get jobs, but they don't keep them. And during an interview, they will share with me dozens of reasons why they couldn't accomplish their goals in those jobs, whether they blame the company for their shortcomings or recount endless personal tragedies (that we all encounter in life) to demonstrate how those supposedly insurmountable obstacles have thwarted their success.

To me, drive is the intellectual and physical energy to get the job done—no matter how high the hurdles or how difficult the hardships. It is a combination of assertiveness, energy, and enthusiasm. Drive is an obvious quality in a highly self-motivated individual. And it's tied to personal mind-set and an enterprising thought process. A person who has a positive attitude and who finds 100 ways to find the 2 ways that work will likely have the drive to get it done. And when I say *energy*, I don't mean the kind possessed by the type-A personality who creates a lot of busy work to appear as if he has drive. I am talking about from-the-gut drive. It is not something you can fake; rather, it is packaged with sincerity because it is a part of the fabric of an individual's soul. Try to fake it and eventually you will be exposed.

So you may recognize that you have drive. But how do you manifest it? You don't want to be a bull in a china shop.

Drive reflects intellect, knowledge, and creativity channeled into positive results, not negative. A person who is goal oriented has drive and is typically focused on his or her objectives. It's someone who can seize an opportunity and leverage it in the most appropriate and professional way.

Innate Curiosity and Common Sense

Innate curiosity and common sense are tremendous influences on one's success in a chosen career and, typically, life in general. People are either born with curiosity and common sense or they're not. You can teach someone the correct questions to ask, but you cannot teach someone to have curiosity about life and the common sense to find her way through it. Call it the nose for news. You either have it, or you don't.

They say curiosity killed the cat, but curiosity doesn't kill professionals—it's a point of differentiation that can fuel success in their careers and can fuel an adventurous life. The notion of curiosity and why some people have it and others don't, why some people leverage it and others don't, is fascinating and telling. Someone who has drive and enthusiasm most certainly has a solid sense of curiosity. If you are curious, you are usually intrigued by the new and different. You'll go out of your way to make discoveries, to acquire knowledge.

Curiosity and common sense work hand in hand. If you don't have the curiosity or the common sense to look for the answer, you better have someone to manage all the details of your life, or you'll be a miserable failure. And this leads me to the commonsense portion of the equation. How you demonstrate common sense and good judgment during the interview process is just as important as the factual information you tell a recruiter. We all make mistakes, and we all have strengths and weaknesses. But there are certain mistakes you might make as a candidate that will eliminate you from the recruiter's consideration, despite your qualifications for a position or the positive impression you have made on the recruiter *prior* to making a serious gaffe. I call this "The Taxi-cab Mentality."

The term *Taxicab Mentality* was born when I was in the process of conducting a search to fill an executive-level position at a Fortune 500 company. One of the professionals whom I wanted to place in the semifinalist panel for this client had difficulty matching his calendar with mine so that I could conduct an in-person interview, which is a critical part of the qualification process. However, because of his stature within his chosen profession and the fact that he had been referred to me by one of the most well-regarded individuals in that same profession, I decided that I would forego the in-person interview, of course informing the client that she would be meeting this candidate without my endorsement of the cultural fit aspect of our counsel. The client agreed and fully understood the logistical conflicts and proceeded to schedule this professional's interviews with the executive team.

The truly disconcerting part of our dealings with this candidate came when he called my firm the day before he was due to travel to the city in which the client company was located. He called and said that his plane was due to arrive at the airport at nearly midnight, and he wanted to know how to find a taxicab! Now, although you may be thinking, "give the candidate a break," stop and realize what an inane question that was. Here was a senior-level executive calling the search firm to inquire about finding a taxicab! That said two things to me as a recruiter: Either he led a privileged life with others always scheduling and doing the mundane (interpret this as "grunt work"), or he was truly highly naïve. Either way, I concluded that his judgment was poor, he was not independent enough in terms of how he conducted himself for our client's culture, and that he simply would not become the top candidate in the search. The latter held true.

Where was his common sense? Where was his good judgment? He exhibited none of these core competencies, and this was a huge issue for me. Remember, success in life is not about being a prima donna and letting the world know through your behavior that you are above it all; it's about good judgment, good judgment, and good judgment! And this leads me to another attribute that I believe is a critical survival quality . . . common sense.

People are born with common sense or they're not. It's a black-and-white issue. It's a genetically rooted attribute. You can teach someone how to approach a situation and how to analyze it, but you can't teach common sense. A few years into my career as a headhunter, I was discussing with an executive my frustration about the fact that most people—probably 75 to 90 percent of the people I encounter—don't have common sense. The executive looked at me and said, "Smooch, stop and think about it—how common is common sense? Have *you* ever asked yourself, How common is common sense? I ask myself that question every single day. It's not at all common." What a great point he made! I'll never forget it, and frankly I am reminded everyday of this notion in my life as a recruiter.

I'll bet some of the greatest mistakes that people make in an interview or in their career have had to do with lack of common sense. You can be the brightest person in the world, but without common sense, you may be mistaken for an imbecile.

Entrepreneur/Intrapreneur

What is the difference between an entrepreneur and an intrapreneur? By definition, an *entrepreneur* is someone who organizes, manages, and assumes the risks of a business or enterprise. An *intrapreneur* is someone who takes that sense of responsibility, accountability, ownership, and drive and leverages it *inside* a company. It's a psychological ownership of the contributions she makes and the counsel that a professional gives to her bosses, colleagues, and subordinates. These individuals are taking entrepreneurial skills and abilities, both literal skill sets and intuitive abilities, and bringing them to the table for their own specific job, their department, and overall to the company where they work. There's a huge difference between the intrapreneurial mind-set and the mind-set of "I am here to punch a clock and collect my paycheck and do the minimal amount of work." The intrapreneur can create structure where none exists, can build a business from the ground up, is always on watch for opportunities, and is goal oriented and future oriented.

When someone is sitting in the executive's chair, opportunities present themselves every day. The executive who does *not* have an intrapreneurial mind-set will put his feet up on the desk, take credit for creating those opportunities, and do nothing to make the most of them. Then there are the professionals who wouldn't recognize an opportunity if it bit them!

More and more every day and further down the employment ladder, senior management seeks individuals with an intrapreneurial mind-set. However, not everyone is comfortable with the notion of being an intrapreneur, as they may confuse it with the characteristics they associate with being an entrepreneur. Keep in mind that an entrepreneur takes a much higher degree of risk than what an intrapreneur would or should take within his company or department. There is a certain risk threshold for every company, and you need to gauge your company's risk tolerance threshold in pursuing your ideas. And remember that the CEO still has the final say, no matter how great your counsel or what level of ownership you take for a function, department, or business unit!

As for the level of risk tolerance with which you might feel comfortable, on a risk-taking scale of 1 to 10, I believe a professional should be somewhere between an 8 and a 9. That's someone who is comfortable taking a measured, calculated crapshoot. Those who rank at 9.5 and above are too high on the scale. Those people are probably willing to risk everything, which then becomes an uncalculated crapshoot. However, I do believe that a high level of comfort associated with risk is critical in a professional. Ranking below a 7 or 8 is undesirable in today's competitive marketplace. Which leads me to risk tolerance ...

Risk Tolerance

Someone who is creative can have an enterprising thought process but may not have the risk tolerance to be an intrapreneur. This brings us to the next core competency: risk tolerance. You will never find success in your career without taking risks. And if we take a risk and fail, we need to pick ourselves up, dust ourselves off, and learn from that failure. What we fear the most is the risk of failing, the risk of losing our job, the risk of looking foolish, particularly to our colleagues and, more specifically, to our boss. But if you don't take that chance, you are doomed to fail anyway and will lose the respect of others—as well as the respect for yourself for not having the guts to stick your neck out.

In today's business world, one's risk tolerance threshold is a huge factor in not just career navigation but in overall professional success. I divide risk tolerance into two categories—the calculated crapshoot and the uncalculated crapshoot. It is the same criterion I used in describing the difference between entrepreneurs and intrapreneurs. A corporate professional should be somewhere between an 8 and 9 in risk tolerance on a scale of 1 to 10.

In today's corporations, more management teams and CEOs in particular are realizing that business and competitive advantage have become so complex and so critical to moving a company forward that they need more people in their employment ranks who are risk tolerant versus risk adverse. Someone who has risk tolerance has courage—not unfounded courage and not bravado, but deeply rooted courage and strong convictions, both a very important part of risk tolerance.

How do recruiters and hiring executives recognize candidates with the appropriate level of risk tolerance? They seek individuals who can counsel CEOs with the right amount of push back. They understand the limits or the corporate culture vis-à-vis push back and risk tolerance. When assessing a candidate, recruiters ask themselves if they believe the professional is comfortable assuming risk or does she play it safe. Does the person have the courage to meet stiff challenges? Is the candidate willing to risk her job by giving direct and honest counsel to the CEO or other senior executives? Ask yourself these questions to determine your level of risk tolerance.

Judgment Calls

I believe the following two questions are critical for professionals to get comfortable with answering when it comes to the concept of judgment calls:

1. What are the really terrific judgment calls you have made in your life, and how did you come to those judgment calls?
2. What are the worst, most disastrous judgment calls you've made, why did you make them, and how did you recover from them?

Recovery is the most important aspect of making a bad judgment call. After all, we're dealing with human capital, and we all make mistakes. And what goes along with human capital is the good, the bad, and the ugly. We all have strengths and weaknesses. You've got to present the whole package. It's the recovery part that's most important in terms of being able to navigate your career forward with any additional depth of understanding or intelligence about how not to repeat those mistakes again. As a recruiter, that's what I'm looking for in a candidate.

Let me give you an example of someone who has grasped that concept. At a recent speaking engagement before members of a professional organization, I was making a point about judgment calls—how important it is to tell your boss what he *needs* to hear versus what he *wants* to hear. I noticed a woman in the audience grinning and nodding her head during this part of the speech. She approached me at the end of my presentation and told me she understands completely the notion of grappling with making the right or wrong judgment call *and* the recovery part of it! She shared with me an incident that happened to her in a very high-profile, senior-level role at the company where she works. She recognized that her CEO was about to move ahead with a plan that would result in him making a $25 million mistake. She had to make a decision: Did she approach the CEO and tell him that she thought the plan he was so proud of had a huge flaw? Doing so could risk her job, her credibility, and her standing with the company. Perhaps she should just shut up, she thought. What was the "right" judgment call? Ultimately, after considerable thought about the situation, she decided she would tell him. She met with him privately and in a very professional manner explained her reasoning and her thinking. He was very unhappy with her taking issue with his grand plan, and it damaged her initially. He went ahead with the program and, indeed, it cost the company and shareholders nearly $25 million.

Here was a professional who knew she was putting her job on the line by taking issue with the CEO, and even though he later acknowledged she was right, she still had to spend some time scratching and clawing her way back to the level of credibility, honor, and trust that she had had prior to telling him. But she made the right judgment call, if for no other reasons than for her own personal psychological well-being as a professional and for her own internal measure of credibility. She was less concerned about how the rest of the world viewed her and more concerned with how well she could sleep at night. To me, that's the epitome of the kind of thinking, mind-set, and approach you want in a professional.

The judgment calls that a professional must make are oftentimes black and white. There is no gray zone in the spectrum. You are either right or wrong. As much as I fundamentally personally like to see that others live in the gray zone because I think it is probably healthier from a psychological standpoint, this is one part of life where there is no gray zone.

What's your track record of impeccable judgment calls in a variety of business situations throughout your own career?

Integrity, Honesty, Credibility, and Trust

A person who possesses these attributes of honor radiates confidence and trust. Integrity cannot be concealed nor faked. Someone who lacks integrity or honesty might attempt to fool recruiters into thinking he is an honest man, and it might be difficult to recognize the fakery at first glance, but it comes out eventually. Discrepancies start showing up. Eventually, it blows up and the sham is exposed.

Throughout my years in executive search, I have been fortunate in that most candidates' references are truthful and clean. However, there have been a couple of exceptions. One such incident involved a candidate who lied about his tenure at a certain company. My client had contacts who had worked at a company at the same time my candidate stated he worked there, and my client said his contact knew of no such person. When I confronted my candidate about this falsehood, he literally squirmed in his seat. I said the only way he would be able to reinstate his credibility and integrity with this client—and with me—was to produce his legal documents that would confirm his employment. They never showed up. Needless to say, his name has been dropped from our list of potential candidates—forever.

Another unfortunate incident involved a candidate who lied about having his undergraduate degree. This candidate was 15 years into a highly successful career. He had a stellar job history. He was a finalist in a search I was conducting for a financial services firm, and for regulatory and securities reasons the company conducts its own background checks, including college degree verification. The company's background check revealed he never graduated from college. Lying about having the degree knocked him out of the search, and as in the case of our other dishonest candidate, knocked him off of my firm's list of target professionals. Had he been forthright in acknowledging that he lacked an academic degree but had the years of experience to perform in the role, my client would have considered his candidacy a strong one and would not have taken issue with this deficiency because his track record spoke for itself.

Remember the adage: "Oh what a tangled web we weave when first we practice to deceive." The notion of creative lying is an oxymoron. In your job search and career, you really need to walk a straight line. If you're caught in a lie, it's near impossible to regain the hiring authorities' confidence in you.

Within your own psyche, how do you stack up? How committed are you as an individual in and of yourself, and to external constituencies, to honesty and integrity? What degree of integrity and credibility do you have among colleagues and within your industry? What value structure issues might you convey?

Business Knowledge

It may be apparent to most professionals that having business knowledge goes without saying. But from my standpoint, there are a lot of things professionals don't do with their business knowledge even though they may bill themselves as the experts. It's one thing to have the knowledge but another thing to know what is useful and how to use it.

You would be surprised at how few business professionals really understand this concept. Let's look at the basics. Most people can rattle off the top of their heads their company's five competitors, but do they really understand those companies' visions? Do they understand how these companies' senior management approaches competitiveness? Do they understand how to leverage that knowledge for their own company's gain? A resounding no to those questions is what I have observed in many candidates I've interviewed over the years.

It should be on every professional's checklist to have a solid understanding of peer companies and of their competitive edges, and to leverage that knowledge for their own company, for their function specifically, and for their overall organization.

Early in my career as a communications professional, prior to my tenure in executive search, I worked for a small but growing public relations agency and then left for another company. My new job turned out to be a career misstep, and ultimately I knew I wanted to return to the agency arena. As I plotted my return, I took four months to interview with every agency in town. If I were fortunate to be hired back with the agency I just left, I would know who the competitors were, how their business was structured, the mind-set and chemistry of the executives and how they approached business, and many other nuggets of marketplace intelligence. And that would have given me (and ultimately did when I went back to the agency), a competitive edge when we were writing new business presentations and pitching new business.

What distinguishes a professional from the masses is how she takes that business knowledge and leverages it in advising senior management or the CEO and in terms of how she can make contributions to areas of their company beyond her own specific function. It also allows her to empower her staff if she manages people. It enables her to be more savvy and knowledgeable with external constituencies. It also can help her in her abilities to recognize and recruit talent. Possessing this kind of business knowledge is essential to building career momentum.

Just having knowledge means nothing in your career. For example, you can know a lot about nothing! At a cocktail party you can be a fountain of trivia and a lot of fun. However, mere volume of knowledge does not necessarily equal the *right* knowledge. You need to take the information and distill it into something useful. You need to define the core pieces of marketplace intelligence that you can leverage within your organization. There's such an information overload right now that it's essential to distill it down to the information that's meaningful. Focus on the meaningful rather than all the other tidbits that are swirling around everyone. That's having and leveraging business knowledge.

Problem-Solving Skills

There are two levels of problem-solving abilities that I think are critical for navigating a successful career. One has to do with the literal, how you develop the equation that solves the problem and what kind of research you do—the actual steps you take to solve the problem. But the other level of problem solving that I believe far outweighs the literal skill set has to do with one's intuitive abilities. In our fast-paced technological society where everything has to happen in a nanosecond, people have to solve problems and make judgment calls on an intuitive level in five seconds or less. One's intuitive ability to be able to sense the answer is critical. In other words, being quick on your feet is crucial to success.

When there is a crisis at a company, the CEO is going to ring in with you and ask, "How do I fix it?" And she is not going to want to hear, "Let me do a six-week study and figure that out for you." Think of it in these terms—*60 Minutes* just landed on your doorstep, and they've got the cameras in the CEO's anteroom. Come on up. And, by the way, there is no back door out of your office. Again, it's a matter of having the right combination of common sense and intuition. In today's corporate America, it's responding as much to the between-the-lines messages as to the tangible ones. It's a radar-and-antenna issue that can be heightened if the marketplace knowledge and business competitiveness are already in one's computerlike mind.

Intuition is one of the most unused, untapped resources that comes packaged inside every human being the second he or she is born. It's a survival skill. And intuition reflects how someone uses creative problem-solving methods to analyze problems, generate options, and make sound judgment calls. Are you intellectually quick, are you fast on your feet, and are you a quick study? It's all about sensing. You might hear someone say something on one level, but there's the between-the-lines part of the conversation that needs to be ferreted out as well. It's the part the conversation or the situation that people need to raise their awareness of and pay more attention to.

Based on the characteristics I've described for a professional who has this problem-solving core competency, what in your career to date would make you stand out from the pack in terms of intellectual and intuitive problem-solving skills?

Proactivity

An enterprising person is proactive. This type of professional takes the initiative. He doesn't wait for something to happen before reacting. Someone who is proactive gets things done. They originate and take action. It's important for you as a professional in your current role and in your career as a whole to have the ability to be proactive in your own efforts, and to motivate others to be proactive. You've seen these professionals on the job. They are skilled at building and maintaining departments or business units. They are comfortable starting something from scratch and designing roles, structures, and processes to achieve corporate goals and objectives. Creative and future oriented, they watch for opportunities to expand and grow. They are typically adaptable and patient, with balanced personalities that enable them to adjust as situations change. And they don't wait for change to react—they anticipate it and have a plan at the ready.

The opposite of a proactive professional is someone who lacks industriousness. This person typically waits for someone else to figure it out. They feel they are entitled to special treatment and typically lack the sustained drive and motivation that is necessary in successful careers. Those who have somehow reached the point of being a senior-level executive without having a proactive nature have done so by overdelegating and taking credit for the projects' successes. Those who are in lower-level management positions and are not proactive feel everything is someone else's job but theirs.

In assessing your career, does your approach to responsibilities embody a forward-thinking, proactive mind-set? Or do you hide behind your title simply reacting to situations when necessary?

Self-Concept

Having a strong self-concept is critical to moving your career forward and to branding your career. I will discuss how you brand yourself and your career in the next chapter, and the key component you need to start with is to know yourself. Knowing yourself is as much as an exercise in maturity as it is walking the paces and the miles of your career. It begins by knowing whom and what you are from a value structure standpoint as a professional as well as knowing your strengths and weaknesses from a technical skill perspective. If your end goal is to be all things to all people, companies, and situations, you will end up navigating a career mediocre in nature. Recognize with conviction what you are all about as a professional and an individual. Know your limitations, your strengths, and your weaknesses and embrace the whole set of factors versus only those that you think will sell your talent.

Is your self-concept healthy and strong enough to intuitively navigate treacherous waters, influence senior management, and develop and motivate staff as though the staff members developed the ideas themselves? Do you have a fundamental respect for people and sensitivity to others' thoughts and opinions, diverse experiences, and backgrounds? Are you a team player? Are you able to express yourself clearly and concisely, through well-written materials and active listening, or are you completely self-absorbed?

Visionary Capabilities

If you are a visionary, you have a global perspective. Even if you are below the level of CEO and the company you work for is small, you must have vision for your business unit, your department, or your function to grow in your career. The core competency of vision is tied to being a proactive individual. Visionaries not only expect the unexpected, they embrace it. They develop winning strategies and tolerate failure as a learning experience. They listen and encourage feedback and are open to new information from others.

These professionals have the imagination to create the big ideas that are grounded in reality and are compelling and relevant to others. They foster a sense of limitless possibilities in what they can accomplish and inspire others to do the same. Key to being a true visionary is how they communicate their vision to others within an organization and how that vision relates to and underscores corporate goals. Otherwise, vision is mere daydreaming. Having vision is what leadership is all about. Someone with vision gets others to take action. Someone who is energetic, committed, and driven—but not a workaholic—has vision. She is not a bull-in-the-china-shop-head-down-and-charge executive. These types don't look up, down, or to the side. That's someone who works without vision. That's someone who just plain can't see!

Do you have the ability to serve as a visionary for your organization or function and inspire others? Are you able to recognize the value of getting ahead of the curve in supporting a company's future direction?

Passion

Passion is my favorite core competency and in my opinion the most important of the 14 intangible attributes. Without passion, it's difficult to imagine someone sustaining the other core competencies for long. When the passion goes away, the other attributes start to fade as well. Passion is rooted deeply in the emotions, as opposed to a drive that's rooted more in intellectual motivation. It's being inwardly inspirational, and that's rooted in the gut. You never challenge it; it's part of your soul. Passion is not about waking up giddy to go to work every morning. It's not just about what you do for a living. When you're passionate, it's an extension of you as an individual. When people are passionate in their career, there's a flow of creativity. It's a channeling of their intellect and a deeper immersion into what they're doing. When I meet candidates who are passionate, they don't need to say they love what they do for a living; it's evident. But watch out for the passion impostors! They claim to be passionate about their work, but dig a little deeper and it will soon be obvious that they're just paying lip service to their emotions. Their feeling of passion is stemming from an intellectual acknowledgment that they are content in their job. That's not true gut-level passion. I've had clients who meet candidates with passion, and they want to hire them on the spot. It's that contagious enthusiasm that makes you want to be on their team. It's the "let's go get 'em" mind-set. It's something that can't be learned. It must come from within. I'll take a passionate junkyard dog over the pedigreed intellectual any day!

So ask yourself: Are you passionate about your profession? Do you wake up in the morning with 100 fresh ideas and a desire to see them to fruition?

Secret: It's not always just about the technical skills or academic knowledge. In the end, the deciding factor is *always* based on intuitive wisdom and intangible qualities. They, after all, supersede everything else.

CHAPTER 8

Branding Your Career
Packaging Yourself for the Recruiter and the Hiring Organization

When you think of packaging yourself for a job interview, what might immediately come to mind is the "dress for success" concept of the 1980s. Dressing for success is largely dead in today's "can you make it happen" world. You might find yourself interviewing for a job in Silicon Valley where T-shirts and jeans are the workplace uniform, whereas a Wall Street job still requires an expensive tailored business suit. There is no standard dress code in today's corporate America. The key is to be appropriately presentable for the environment.

Dress codes aside, the point you must understand today is how to package, or brand, yourself with recruiters and the hiring organization to move your career forward. Employers recognize that it's what's inside that counts. No one is hiring empty suits. You must demonstrate that you actually lived the successes that you profess to have experienced in your resume. After all, you may initially buy the box of Wheaties because you like its cover and the athlete endorsing the product, but you also have to like what's inside the package, or you won't return to the store for more.

How do you brand your career to differentiate yourself from the thousands of professionals who have similar experience and credentials as you and who have also sent their resume to recruiters or prospective employers? You may think, who needs to worry about that? In today's job market I don't need to sell myself—it's a candidate's employment market—there are more jobs than there is talent to fill those positions, which makes career navigation easy. *Wrong assumption!*

Allow me to make one point very clear: The candidate may have owned the labor market in recent years because of the technology boom and an overall sense of prosperity. However, the searing hot economy of the late 1990s and most of the year 2000 has cooled, and the job market has cooled along with it. I'd like to share with you some startling statistics of what the shape of the job market might look like in the future. According to a recent article in *Time* magazine titled "The Twilight of the Boomers," the 76 million post–World War II baby boomers are competing for jobs with their children, the echo-boomers. The author of the article, Daniel Okrent, states that "there are plenty of smart, energetic 33-year-olds who are more than eager to step into the shoes of every smart, not-so-energetic 53-year-old—for less money too, and probably with more appropriate new-economy skills. And the echo-boomers will end up likely caring for their folks, who may run out of money during their retirement years." And, the article continues, "A strapped nation may have to choose between caring for its children or its parents. Today there are 3.4 wage-earning (and Social Security contributing) American workers for every person over 65. In 2030 there will be only two workers for each of the elderly. Those two are either going to have to work a lot harder to support all the old folks, or we will see a spectacle of misery unprecedented in the world's wealthiest nation."

Regardless of the state of the economy, the job market, or to what generation you belong, you need to manage your career and be prepared for potential changes under any circumstances. If you do, you will weather any economic shift or employment climate far better if you are a well-known brand than an unknown entity! Let's review some of the best-known brands, examine the general principles of branding, and then identify ways in which you may apply those principles to your career.

Brand Category Killers—What Is a Brand?

A category killer outsells, outpaces, and outdoes its competition in every way by having a strong brand. Although there are numerous recognizable brands in every category, the category killers stand out from among the pack, and you know what they are: Coke and Pepsi; Procter & Gamble, Gillette, and Johnson & Johnson; Kleenex; GM and Ford; Mercedes, BMW, Lexus, and Honda; Levi's and The Gap; Starbucks; Nike and Adidas; McDonald's and Burger King; Ralph Lauren and Gucci; Rolex; General Electric, Maytag and Whirlpool; General Mills and Quaker Oats; Absolut, Budweiser, and Corona; Intel, Hewlett-Packard, IBM, Apple, and Dell; Nokia; Yahoo! and AOL; AT&T; Disney; Sony; Martha Stewart; Oprah/Harpo Productions; American Airlines, United Airlines, and the Boeing Company; Visa and American Express—and the list goes on.

Just look at what you are wearing right now. You are probably a walking advertisement for some of the best-known brands. Look around your house at your furnishings. You probably purchased a certain model appliance based on the qualities of the brand—its reliability and performance, not just the color. What kind of computer and printer do you use, and did you make your purchase based on its capabilities or its size and shape or both? Look in your garage. Did you buy a family car for reliability or a dream car for excitement? In music, many performers are more than just musicians—they are world-renowned brands. You need only to mention the first name of some and it evokes tremendous emotion. Madonna. Cher. The Beatles. Elvis. Britney Spears. 'N Sync. These professionals have spawned huge brands through music videos and merchandise, over and above the popularity of their recordings. And what about entertainers such as Arnold Schwarzenegger, Julia Roberts, Meg Ryan, Bruce Willis, and Tom Hanks? Not to mention the Worldwide Wrestling Federation and what it has done to marketing and branding. These celebrities have become brands that have generated huge merchandise revenues. All of these category killers know what it takes to attract consumers and keep them over the years. They squash the competition. There are corporate brands, family brands, individual brands, and subbrands. Similarly, your goal is to become a category killer in your industry or functional discipline—and yes, in your career.

Fundamentals of Branding— What Constitutes a Brand?

According to the worldwide branding consulting firm Landor Associates, whose credits include the branding strategies for corporate leaders such as Lucent, FedEx, Hewlett-Packard, and ITT Industries, the following fundamental truths govern branding:

1. To be successful, a brand must consistently provide quality and satisfaction.
2. It must meaningfully distinguish itself from the competition to create customer preference.

3. It must be relevant, convenient, and easily accessible to its target audience, and it must appeal to their individual lifestyles, attitudes, and beliefs.

To be certain, a brand provides a level of quality, trust, convenience, assurance, and allure for which customers are willing to pay a premium. And the brand must be successfully communicated to a target audience.

Brands must also have longevity. They establish their worth, build on it, and evolve or reinvent themselves to satisfy their consumer or audience. They must maintain high standards, raising the bar when the competition approaches that standard. If they rest on their laurels and don't reinvent the brand to stay current or at least continue to speak to the target audience, they will surely lose market share. A brand must also transcend cultural barriers and communicate to multiple consumer segments. Coke and Pepsi are consumed worldwide and need only translate their list of ingredients into other languages, not change their packaging, to appeal to multiple cultures. A great brand evokes emotion. After all, emotions drive our decision-making process. When you give something wrapped in a classic robin's-egg-blue Tiffany box, the recipient of the gift will likely experience a range of emotions and expectations. You knew this when you bought the gift. If the recipient of the gift opens the box and its content is something other than precious, like an old shoe, he will likely feel tremendous disappointment and cheated—not to mention be very unhappy with the giver! The brand should consistently represent and deliver a certain standard of quality and value. You don't want any negative surprises associated with the brand. You should be able to trust that the brand will offer the value it communicates. A brand also should be relevant. If you don't want it, you won't buy it. It needs to meet your needs and/or wants. It needs to keep its promise to you, the consumer. If it keeps that promise, you will be loyal to the brand. Loyalty is another key component to the creation of a brand.

Applying Branding Fundamentals to Yourself and Your Career

How can you apply these hallmarks of traditional branding to your career? In a job search or in your career, you are the product. The variables that define you as a product are your education, your work experience, and your intangible attributes. You need to package these variables and then position yourself in the job market by marketing these variables through the fundamentals of branding. To accomplish this, I recommend you focus on the following key principles:

1. **Candidate, Know Thyself:** Identify the competitive advantages that comprise your brand. What are your skills, your strengths, your weaknesses, and your passions? What differentiates you from the hordes of other candidates in the marketplace? How do you make yourself attractive to prospective employers?

2. **Candidate, Know Thy Competition:** Identify the talent base of your competition and what qualities they possess that you may have or don't have. And identify what corporations find desirable in a candidate and emphasize the qualities and experience you have that match the requirements; find ways to strengthen those skills or requirements that you lack.

3. **Candidate, Know Thy Audience:** Identify your target audience and how your competitive advantages address their needs. How will you add value to an organization, both in the short and long term?

4. **Candidate, Know How to Communicate to Thy Audience:** Effectively communicate and deliver your brand to the market. How do you package yourself and your credentials, and what tools can you employ to best communicate your key messages to a recruiter and/or prospective employer?

Let's examine each of these professional branding points in depth.

152

Candidate, Know Thyself—What Do You Want to Be When You Grow Up?

Branding yourself is as much an exercise in maturity as it is walking the paces and the miles of your career. Branding begins by knowing who and what you are from a value structure standpoint as a professional as well as knowing your strengths and weaknesses from a technical skill perspective. If your end goal is to be all things to all people, companies, and situations, you will end up navigating a career that is mediocre in nature. Recognize with conviction what you are all about as a professional and an individual. Know your limitations, your strengths, and your weaknesses, and embrace the whole set of factors versus only those that you think will sell your talent. Also critical to recognize is that in the first decade or so in your career, you may not know yet what your end goal is or the path that you want to take, but know well what you don't know. You need to know the product before you can market it.

Let me give you an example of why it is so important to know yourself as a candidate. Oftentimes my clients will ask me to conduct a courtesy interview with a particular professional whom they believe could use some career guidance. And as a matter of course I'm always pleased to spend the time working with professionals to help them navigate more productive and satisfying career paths. However, invariably when sitting across the table from someone, early on in the conversation I'll ask her about such things as industry preferences and what are the top two or three industries in which she would prefer to work. And with great conviction, the response always comes back, "I could work in any industry." As the conversation continues and we traverse across a variety of subjects all related to her career, I come back to that question of industry preference, but I approach it from a different perspective. I ask the professional about a specific industry, for example, manufacturing. And at that juncture there is an unequivocal and resounding, "Oh, I could *never* work in manufacturing!" At that point in the conversation, it becomes apparent to me that one, this professional either doesn't know herself very well or two, she hasn't put one ounce of thought to the subject matter, or three, she is attempting to brand or market herself for every potential opportunity known to the employment marketplace.

It is at this point in counseling candidates that I embark upon a heart-to-heart discussion and encourage them to gain some objectivity about themselves and their career and to understand fully how they are packaging and branding themselves to their *detriment*. Toward this end, I recommend that you identify the top five qualities—both skill sets and intangible leadership assets—that best showcase who you are as a professional and how you can best add value to an organization.

Equally important as knowing what you want in defining your brand is for you to acknowledge and understand the circumstances or situations in which you would never want to be involved. Every one of us has a handful of experiences from various points in our careers that we would be loath to go through again. One of the most critical thought processes to go through in defining a career brand is to know well which types of situations you would never want to be involved in again under any circumstances. Is it the CEO that's a screamer? Is it the boss that pounds his fist? Or is it the colleague who continually chastises her peers in the department for their lack of perfection and attention to detail?

Another point critical to knowing thyself would be operating environment characteristics that are acceptable to you. One such example has to do with the new economy and the fact that the media conveys to us that all future operating environments will have the same characteristics as the dot-coms: 24/7 and how many beepers, cell phones, and pagers can you wear on your belt so that you can be at your boss's beck and call. Truth be told, is that really the operating environment in which you want to place yourself? Perhaps it is, perhaps not. What's important is for you to know what's best for you. It reminds me of a candidate we interviewed on behalf of a dot-com client whose career roots were based in more traditional, conservative companies. When I interviewed him, I recognized that he had a high degree of intellectual capital and appeared to be enterprising and passionate about his chosen profession. However, when we continued our dialogue about broader career issues beyond the specific position for which I was interviewing him, he revealed to me that he was exploring a handful of additional opportunities as well. And guess what the nature of those operating environments was? You guessed it—all conservative and traditional in their orientation. And although I could see him making the leap to the dot-com world with an initial severe dose of shock, in reality, his comfort level was with a non-24/7, more traditional working environment.

One of the lessons to be learned as you go down this path of defining your brand is that you also need to recognize where the pendulum should balance between three key factors—career, personal professionalism, and one's personal life. Be certain to discern the best and worst circumstances in structuring the components of your career brand. Don't try to be all things to all people, companies, and situations. Recognize that you might not know what it is you are chasing. Key to this is to acknowledge five circumstances or situations in which you would never want to be involved.

Candidate, Know Thy Competition— Understanding the Talent Base

When you are initially attempting to define your own personal career brand, it is important that you understand the broader landscape of talent against which you are competing. For example, within your industry, what are the backgrounds and profiles of your peers at competitor organizations? Within your category of academic achievement, whether it's undergraduate, MBA, or Ph.D., what are the paths those professionals have navigated in terms of careers? In your attempt to define your brand, you are looking for marketplace clues that provide you with some insight to help you determine whether to choose a brand that is more common in corporate America or to define a unique brand for yourself.

Another avenue of research that you must pursue is to examine what corporations want and need in a candidate, now and over the long term. Included in this category would be the CEO's and senior management's expectations and desires of practitioners in your particular profession as well as the historic and current career discipline trends and how you can interpret those for future use in your career. For example, over the course of my career in headhunting in the communications discipline, I've witnessed a change of opinion as to who has the edge in this profession, the specialist or the generalist.

Another critical area that must be considered in your effort to define your career brand has to do with both technical skills as well as intangible leadership qualities. And as you conduct your research, talk with colleagues within your chosen profession, and examine market place factors, you need to begin to get your arms around what the driving factors of success are. Remember, one of the greatest trends that has gained significant energy and speed in the past few years has been this intangible notion of leadership qualities. As I discussed in the prior chapter, intangible assets are as much a factor in defining your brand as they are to leading your overall career success.

Once you've completed the fact finding and gathering of information, take some time to synthesize it, gain some objectivity, and step back and think what is pertinent and germane to you as an individual. Identify your desired and intended career goals and begin sifting or culling out those facts and factors that strike a positive chord with you. At this point you should have a good sense of your professional brand identity as it compares to that of your competition, so begin leveraging your brand to navigate your career. And if you recognize that you lack some of the skill set strengths and intangible qualities of your competition, take proactive steps to develop or enhance your abilities in those areas. Match and evolve your skills to the market's needs today and in the future.

Candidate, Know Thy Audience—Who Am I Targeting?

Your obvious target for a job search or career-branding campaign would be a prospective employer. If you are a college professor, you would target your credentials to an institute of higher learning. If you are a physician, you would target a well-respected hospital or medical practice. A marketing professional would aim for a top spot in a corporation in an industry or marketing agency that she prefers. Who else is your target audience? Headhunters, of course. And so is virtually *everyone* in your professional life (and some in your personal life). Everyone with whom you have contact should recognize your brand. Remember that you are not immune to judgment from all people. It's common sense, but if you are a candidate or someone on a career track, it's critical to recognize that in shaping your brand, the world is your audience. It's how you behave in traffic, at social functions, in restaurants—everywhere you go, people are watching you. They form an opinion about how you behave, how you carry yourself, what you say, and to whom you say it. It's unavoidable for people to withhold judgment about you and your character. Why? It's human nature.

I'm sure you've heard stories about candidates or vendors driving to a job interview with a prospective employer or meeting with a potential client and having a confrontation on the road only to arrive at the destination and realize the other driver was the person with whom they were meeting! Would you hire someone who cut you off in traffic and then swore at you, shaking his fist? Would you feel comfortable with a candidate's judgment if you saw her at a restaurant, possibly after "a few too many," making a scene? Although you don't want to compromise your personal freedom, style, or opinion, even with six billion people the world is still small, and it is wise to err on the side of caution.

How important is it for you to brand your career? If you don't brand yourself, you can bet people will brand you themselves! You see it every day. And you undoubtedly brand others yourself. Think about it. You might say to a colleague, "I don't want to give Peter that project because he's a procrastinator. He'll never get it done." Or "Jennifer's strategies are so creative. She can come up with one hundred ways to solve a problem." He's lazy, she's proactive, that team is productive—these identifiers are constantly branding someone. Do you want people to brand you with qualities that you don't believe portray you in the best light? Do you want to be seen as lacking in certain areas that you know are your strengths but you just haven't had a chance to prove them? The answer is no unless you want to fail miserably in your career. You are not immune to judgment by others.

Even though the whole world is potentially your audience for your brand, you need to narrow it down for purposes of either securing a position or defining your brand with your present employer. You will want to target each segment a little differently and employ specific methods or tools that are appropriate for each. If you are a job seeker, you need to identify prospective employers, executive recruiters, and networking contacts with whom to brand yourself. Ideally, you have developed and nurtured over the years a network of professionals and individuals on whom you can rely to help you spread the word that you are in the job market. You will want to be certain that they are current with what your brand represents. Reconnect with those who may not know of your most recent accomplishments or area of expertise. As I mentioned before, someone will know someone who knows you. If that individual knows a prospective employer you have targeted and he mentions your name and the other individual doesn't realize you have certain expertise, he may raise doubt in the hiring authority's mind that you are indeed qualified for an opportunity. Always keep your network of contacts apprised of your current employment and latest accomplishments.

If you are employed at present, you want to ensure you maintain high visibility inside your organization with supervisors (both direct and indirect), peers, and subordinates. Although it's important to increase their awareness of you in the company, you also want to ensure that their knowledge of your capabilities is accurate. If a member of senior management sees you performing only in one very limited capacity and your skill set is much broader, make an effort to change her perception of your abilities and your brand. To all audiences, your goal is to become a known entity in your area of expertise. Let's see how you might accomplish this goal.

Candidate, Know How to Communicate to Thy Audience— Your Resume Is Only the Beginning

So you've decided what you want to be when you grow up, you know your strengths and limitations, you recognize your competition, and you know whom you want to target for your branding campaign. You're on the right path to defining your brand. The next strategy that needs to come into play is directly tied to marketing your brand. Anyone involved in marketing a product knows that whether it's soap or cars, it must distinguish itself from among the hundreds of other "me-too" items on the shelf. It needs to shout *buy me!* Similarly, if you are a job seeker, you want to communicate to your audience *hire me!* How do you, the "product," best market your brand?

Just as in a successful marketing or advertising campaign, you want to create the highest number of impressions through the appropriate media to ensure you will reach your target audience. To market your brand as a candidate or an employee seeking to strengthen your brand, there are numerous media you will want to deploy. For the candidate, your resume and cover letter are your primary means to branding your career with recruiters and prospective employers. How long and in what format should your resume and cover letter be? You could ask 100 people that same question and get 100 different answers. However, there are some key guidelines to follow in preparing your resume, and most of the 100 people should agree on many of them. Let me offer some guidelines to writing a resume that will be impactful and support your branding effort:

1. *Length:* Hiring executives and recruiters do not have much time to review lengthy resumes. Most agree a 20-second scan is about all each resume in the pile will receive. It should be as persuasive as possible and entice the reader to want to know more. In general, you want to make your qualifications clear to the reviewer and be succinct without sacrificing your key points. Limiting a resume to two pages is the general rule. If you believe two pages won't do your career justice, enclose an addendum of accomplishments you feel is critical for the prospective employer to know. This addendum can be tweaked appropriately for the type of position you are seeking.

2. *Format:* Organize your resume in a legible and logical format. It should be easy for the reader to immediately identify who you are, where you live, and what your area of expertise is. You want to ensure that in the first scan the hiring authority knows how to reach you if he is interested. Some candidates list incorrect or leave out important and complete contact information. Include your full name (include Mr. or Ms. for names that could be either gender), home address, home, work and cell phone numbers, and e-mail addresses. I recommend following this with a career objective so that the reader will immediately recognize what you do for a living. This is typically two or three lines of copy. Follow this by a chronological—present to past—documentation of your work experience. Don't make your career a mystery by giving a vague summary of your capabilities. And don't exclude any gaps in your experience—your career path is what it is! Remember, we all have gaps in our careers at one point or another, and it is perfectly acceptable. Make it easy to read and relevant to the position you are seeking. Include the full name of your company, its location, and a line

about what it does, annual revenues, and number of employees. Even if the company you work for is a household name, you want to ensure that the details of its size and scope are known to the reader.

Your full title and length of time employed with the company should be listed, followed by both your responsibilities and your accomplishments. Let me emphasize the *accomplishments* part of your resume. A key part of your branding effort is not only *what* you did but also *how* you did it. Include any relevant and impressive figures, promotions, and to whom you reported. Your most recent 10 years of employment in this format will suffice, with a brief summary of your prior work experience.

Include your college education, complete with name of the institution, academic degrees received, majors, and the years you graduated. Many prospective employers require degree verification as part of reference checking, so including that information will expedite that process. If you fear age discrimination, you need to get past that barrier at some point during the course of interviewing. Be honest and forthright in presenting your academic information, including dates, and if you are an enthusiastic, well-qualified professional, you will present yourself in an interview as ageless.

3. *Personal information:* You will hear a number of different opinions on whether to include marital status, children, hobbies, and other information beyond your professional experience. My suggestion: Use good judgment and prudence. If you are particularly proud of your accomplishments outside your work life, include them. Hiring managers assume that candidates who have reached a certain point in their careers are committed to succeeding in their profession of choice. Outside interests and family have not impeded your progress in the past, and they likely won't in the future.

4. *Salary information and references:* Including this on a resume is not necessary. The recruiter or hiring executive will ask for this information when it's appropriate during the interview process. Your well-written resume should emphasize your accomplishments and speak to your level of experience. Including salary history and high-profile references along with your resume may appear to be boastful.

5. *Key words:* Everyone talks about including certain key words for scanners—human or computerized—to read. In my opinion, key words in your resume should serve to emphasize your brand. If you include language that is relevant to your strengths and accomplishments and address how you meet the requirements of the position you are seeking, including key words from someone's trumped-up list won't ensure your resume is chosen from the hundreds. A well-written, relevant document will.

6. *Colored paper, designs, font style, photos:* Your goal is to have your resume be as easy to read as possible. Why would you distract from this goal by printing your resume on dark or patterned paper and using a fussy font style? Please, print your resume on light-colored paper—white or cream—as it is easier to read and copies well. Today, we receive more resumes via e-mail, so that issue may be laid to rest forever! And please, no decorations, photos, or other such embellishments. Keep your font style simple, consistent, businesslike, and easy to read. And as I mentioned in Chapter 6, *do not include your photo (or any photos) with your resume.* You want to be hired based on the merits of your career accomplishments, not your appearance.

7. *Typos:* I can't tell you how many resumes I've seen from candidates who are "mangers." Please be sure your resume is free of typos and grammatical errors. Have a trusted colleague proof your resume—better yet, actually use the spell and grammar check features that nearly all software programs offer! Remember, recruiters and

hiring executives receive hundreds of resumes a day and are looking for ways to eliminate candidates. Often resumes will undergo a process whereby administrative assistants will cull through them and weed out as many of the unqualified as possible to save the executives time. If the support staff has been instructed to toss resumes with typos, would you want to risk having a "manger" or two on your all-important document?

8. *Cover letter:* A cover letter is important to include along with your resume. First, it should tell the reader who you are and why you are sending him your resume. What is your purpose or intent in writing? Are you interested in a particular position that you know is available at the company? Or are you seeking an informational interview? The cover letter also should serve as a general introduction to your and your background. A quick paragraph summarizing this information is sufficient. This letter should serve as a brief selling tool and pique the reader's interest to learn more about you by reading your resume. Don't underestimate the power of your cover letter. Also, if the hiring executive wants to learn more about you, be sure your contact information is included on your letter in the event your resume becomes separated from this critical brand/marketing document.

There are shelves and shelves of books on resume writing for you to peruse and and from which you can choose a style that best meets your criteria in your job search or branding effort. In general, your resume should provide a well-rounded look at your professional life—the brand and how you can add value to an organization. It should also be honest and forthright in conveying your work experience. If you expand your accomplishments and capabilities, it will take the recruiter or hiring executive minutes to expose those untruths. So don't do it! Be truthful in presenting your qualifications and background.

Now, let's look beyond your resume as a means to communicating your brand to your target audiences.

For the candidate as well as presently employed individuals, to fully brand yourself and your career, it is critical to *raise your profile in the business world*. Allow me to reiterate from Chapter 4 my suggestions for increasing your visibility among recruiters as well as others whom are likely to be your target audience in your professional branding campaign:

- Join industry associations and professional organizations and become an active member—*network*.
- Initiate speaking engagements in forums appropriate and relevant to your profession or industry. Be viewed as a cutting-edge thought leader.
- Write articles in industry trade and professional publications or other such journals, and if and when published, send the articles to recruiters and professional contacts you feel might serve to advance your career.
- Become well known to coworkers both within and outside your department by taking the initiative on high-visibility projects as well as supporting colleagues in their endeavors.
- Be active in your community. Support nonprofit organizations relevant to your work and participate in fund-raising activities and events.
- Send your resume to a targeted list of recruiters.

Shop 'til You Drop

Although I stated earlier that the world is your audience in your branding campaign, don't misinterpret that as meaning every opportunity is yours to seek if you market yourself as a brand. You don't want to shop opportunities. What do I mean by *shopping*? There is a notion in the search industry that's called "shopping opportunities." It basically means that you are going to be much like the professional I referred to earlier in the chapter, that you are going to want to try on every size, shape, and definition of career opportunity. This is one of the most unacceptable and unprofessional methodologies of career navigation in the marketplace. After all, if you know who you are and have a well-defined brand as a candidate, you should be highly selective about when you are going to agree to participate in an executive search process and when you are not. Navigating your career is not like shopping for your next business suit. Don't tease the recruiter or other hiring authority with insincere interest in an opportunity when you know it is not an industry that interests you or a geographic area where you would consider relocation. Shopping opportunities is not a wise strategy in terms of marketing your brand. You want to be highly discerning, tighten up your criteria and reasons for being interested in a position, and make sure that the potential opportunity meets most of your expectations before moving forward or expressing interest.

———

Secrets: Branding tip of a lifetime: BRAND YOUR TALENT! Bill Gates didn't become a legend by waiting for someone else to create the ideas or the venture cap firms to throw money at him. So what are you waiting for? You deserve to be as well branded as the most successful technology and consumer packaged goods companies in the world. Branding isn't just acceptable for products anymore.

CHAPTER 9

Interviewing Magic
The Taboos and Techniques of the Job Interview

For many, the job interview ranks as high up on the stress chart as some well-known fears and phobias, such as public speaking, flying, spider encounters, or a trip to the dentist. It can be among the more stressful situations you will ever experience. But it doesn't have to be. You can turn a job interview into a positive, stimulating experience that will get you the results you seek. Although not every interview may result in a job offer, when you conduct yourself in a professional, engaging, and honest manner, you can bet that the recruiter will keep you among those at the top of her list for the next great opportunity.

How many of you have been through an intensive job interview process more than once or twice? As a successful midcareer professional—with 10 or 12 years of work experience—your interviewing experience is probably pretty limited. You may have accepted one or two courtesy or exploratory interviews with a recruiter or interviewed in earnest for an opportunity and were not moved forward in the search process. In short, you might have had only a handful of interviews up to the midpoint in your career. So, you may think, how can you possibly be expected to know what to say or how to behave in an interview if you haven't had some coaching? After all, how many professional interviewees are there in the world? Zero, as far as I know. If there are any professional interviewees out there, they are either paid by a research firm to study how people behave in an interview or they are professional candidates who somehow land interviews but never the job! Recruiters don't want to meet professional interviewees. They want to meet candidates who are sincere, exude confidence and credibility, engage the interviewer, and provide him with the information needed to move your candidacy forward. If you employ these basics, you will sense your interviewing magic at work.

Even with limited interviewing experience, so much of how you respond in an interview should be grounded in plain common sense. In prior chapters I shared with you the mechanics of the search process and interviewing etiquette, and now I'd like to give you *my* perspective on some classic, time-worn interviewing techniques and taboos about which most headhunters and human resource professionals will expect you to know.

The Handshake

Everyone appreciates a warm, open greeting with a heartfelt handshake. It tells so much about your people skills and confidence. Although I would not necessarily rule out a candidate based solely on his handshake, the professional who gives me an appropriately firm grip will score higher on a first-impression basis than the candidate who gives me a weak, three-fingertip, limp-wristed, cold-fish, barely-want-to-make-contact handshake. And more often than not, style of handshake is an indication of the candidate's self-concept. A strong handshake is an expression of enthusiasm for meeting someone; a weak one conveys disinterest, whether intentional or not. If the candidate is not enthusiastic about getting together with me or learning more about an opportunity, why is he there in the first place? By *strong handshake* I don't mean an eye-popping vise grip. I've had both men and women express a bit too much enthusiasm for the interview and give me a bone-crushing greeting. Find a happy medium between the cold-fish and vise-grip handshake.

Look Me in the Eye

Eye contact is a critical part of your overall communication skills and professional demeanor. You should be cognizant of good eye contact when carrying on a conversation with anyone in a business setting and even in social situations. It's polite to make good eye contact. However, because you have such a brief time frame to connect with an interviewer, meaningful eye contact becomes even more important. You want to ensure your point is being made as well as to demonstrate that you are a good listener. I don't mean that you should be staring someone down during the interview, but you should be looking at the interviewer, not out the window, at the desktop, at the pictures on the wall, or down at your hands. Good eye contact, along with appropriate eye breaks and head nodding, is acknowledgment that you are an active participant in the discussion. There are some exceptions, however, to this rule. In certain cultures it is impolite to look someone in the eye when you are speaking, but not in corporate America. In general, if you have a shifty-eyed manner, you may not be able to develop the level of trust with the interviewer that is critical to being considered an appropriate candidate for a specific position.

Body Language

When all eyes are upon you in an interview, everything you do and say is taken into consideration to formulate a decision on your candidacy, including how you sit, stand, move your hands, smile, and cross your legs. It's all fair game in the evaluation process. Just look at the presidential debates as an example. Reporters chastised Governor George W. Bush for smirking, pursing his lips, fidgeting in the chair, and head ducking and Vice President Al Gore for being wooden, sighing deeply, and rolling his eyes. No candidate is above being judged about his body language.

During the interview, be conscious of your movements. Following the handshake, lower yourself into the chair gracefully and sit down with an open, receptive posture. Sit up in the chair or toward the front as you will appear more alert, self-confident, and enthusiastic than if you are slumping into it. Be aware of nervously fidgeting with your hair or eyeglasses or picking at your cuticles. You also should acknowledge personal space and not get too close to the interviewer. A candidate who was in a search that our firm was not conducting once told me he was ruled out by the hiring executive because he put his elbow on the executive's desk and the interviewer thought he was too comfortable and familiar. The candidate said he would not have wanted to work for someone that sensitive anyway! Although being ruled out as a candidate for that reason might seem trivial, it demonstrates a point that body language sends a message to an interviewer. How that person might interpret that message can eliminate you as a candidate, even if it appears to be unfair and rather shallow.

Dress Code

Prior to the 1990s' introduction of "business casual," most professionals never questioned what to wear to an executive-level job interview. For men, it was black, navy, or gray wool business suits; a conservative tie; a white shirt; and lace-up shoes. For women, it was a classic, dark business suit with a skirt, modest in length; low-heeled pumps; a silk blouse; a strand of pearls; and quiet earrings. Although dress codes have become less restrictive in corporate America, in an interview situation I strongly recommend that candidates err on the more formal side in their apparel selection. Also, keep your shoes and briefcase shined, your nails manicured, and your hair neat. Men, please remember to wear long, dark socks. I recently had a client complain that she loved the candidate but could I please suggest that he buy some long socks for the meeting with the CEO?

What you wear conveys a message. You want to show the prospective employers that you understand that as a representative of their company you must represent them appropriately. If you are interviewing for a position with a Midwest manufacturing company, you will presumably dress more conservatively than when you interview with a New York City fashion house. Lack of a dress code can be confusing for candidates. Without rules to follow, professionals can often end up looking ridiculous, such as by pairing heavy cotton sports socks with dress shoes and slacks, or just plain sloppy and unkempt. How you dress matters to the interviewer, perhaps more than it should. Don't delude yourself that you may be immune to a 30-second impression based on what you are wearing. We're all human and subject to forming an opinion of you based on your choice of attire. The general rule is to look sharp and appropriately dressed for an executive at the organization.

Rule number one in deciding what to wear to an interview is to be clean and pressed and look sharp and businesslike. Demonstrate that you could be an executive at the company where you are interviewing. A guideline to follow is what the executives at the company wear when they attend a business meeting outside the offices. Suppose the CEO wears khakis and a sports shirt or casual blouse and slacks in the office but a business suit to a media interview or photo session for the annual report; if so, you should wear business attire. The hiring executives want to see you at your best. As a potential representative of the company, what would you wear to meet a customer, a reporter, security analysts, or a potential business partner? That's what I would recommend for an interview with the client (or recruiter), unless you are specifically asked by the interviewer to dress otherwise.

Can I Offer You Something to Drink?

When meeting a recruiter or the client executives in their offices, you will be offered something to drink as a courtesy. I once had a candidate say that she learned she should accept whatever refreshment she is offered in a job interview. I don't know who told her that, but I suspect it was either her mother or a recruiter. If someone offers you coffee or water and it looks convenient for them to bring it to you, you may want to accept. If you don't want anything to drink or you are concerned that you will spill it on yourself or the interviewer, don't feel obliged to do so! Often candidates will want and need liquid refreshment because they get parched during an interview from talking or from nervousness. A warm drink will help soothe your throat muscles if tight better than a cold one.

Small Talk

Employ common sense as your guideline when making small talk in an interview situation. When you first meet the recruiter or hiring executives, you want a brief period of light conversation as a transition into the nuts-and-bolts interview. It's a nice "get to know you" period. Keep small talk light and away from negative subjects. You don't want to drone on about the awful flight, bad weather, or your fitful night's sleep. You want to establish rapport with the interviewer, but don't offer canned comments or stilted compliments as a way to do so. The interviewer will see right through it. A genuine comment about the company, the offices, or the people you meet is just fine. If you feel comfortable remarking on the items the interviewer has in his office, that, too, is acceptable "ice breaker" talk. Stay away from politics, religion, or other subjects that can elicit strong opinions on the part of the interviewer or you—risky territory. Not only is it inappropriate in the interview setting, but it also might position you as someone whose focus is more on these outside interests than the opportunity at hand, and you may be branded a maverick. If the executive does not respond to your small-talk overtures, this is your cue to cut it short.

Talking Too Much

My advice during an interview: Stay focused. One of the most common complaints from clients is that candidates talk too much during an interview. Finding a balance between talking too much and too little can sometimes be difficult for candidates because, after all, talking is what you do in an interview! And you are specifically there to market your brand. But today's executives are more interested in a 50–50 dialogue between the interviewer and the candidate. Give the interviewer a chance to ask you questions and share some of her own philosophy on the subject. I had one client tell me that he met with someone for two hours and only asked three questions; the rest of the time the candidate talked. Part of the responsibility of the interviewer is to be able to manage the conversation to get a word in edgewise. However, not all executives are effective interviewers. In fact, one of my client executives had a candidate fall asleep during the interview! What recruiters and hiring executives want to see in a candidate—and a potential employee—is the ability to answer questions thoughtfully, succinctly, and clearly and to have a point of view. Candidates should be able to explain a complex issue with ease and not get bogged down in too much detail. You should communicate your vision, your accomplishments, and your strategic approach supported by facts, but only enough facts to make your point, not spin a yarn.

You also want to be cognizant of overusing the word *I* in presenting your accomplishments. Executives want a team player, and it's good form to punctuate your presentation with *we* and *my team*. And a word of caution: Don't gossip about your boss or colleagues or reveal confidential or classified information. It shows the interviewer only that you can't be trusted and that perhaps you don't respect the notion of confidentiality, which becomes more and more critical as your career tenure increases. You don't want to be cagey about answering questions, but know when to draw the line and tell the interviewer that because of confidentiality issues, you don't feel comfortable sharing certain information. The interviewer will understand and respect your integrity.

Saying Too Little

One-word or one-line answers are just as bad as giving someone an hour-long spiel in response to a question. To me it can be worse because you don't learn anything about the candidate except that he cannot communicate properly. Although you want to allow the interviewer time to ask questions and give her own perspective on a topic, you need to get across to her what differentiates you from the other candidates and what will make the executive want to hire you. That's the end goal. If you don't make a case for yourself, who will? I've had candidates take an attitude that everything I might want to know about him is in the resume. In fact, when I've asked candidates certain questions, some look at me as if I have two heads. Then they gesture to their resume in front of me and smirk that it's all right there; didn't I read it? Well, yes, I did read it. That's probably what made me pick up the phone and call you. However, I want to bring your resume to life. I want to hear an engaging story about your work history directly from you, not just learn about it from a piece of paper. Market your career brand! Make it interesting. Make it come alive. This is your opportunity to shine. Without being arrogant, boast a little about your accomplishments. If you don't, who will?

Is Silence Golden or a Test?

Silence in an interview or a conversation in general can be awkward and uncomfortable. Two people sitting in silence makes it appear as though you and the person with whom you are speaking have nothing in common and nothing to say to each other. However, a job interview is not a blind date. It's not a social occasion, period. It's a period of time during which you and the hiring executive are exchanging information and becoming more familiar with one another for the purposes of deciding if the executive is going to hire you and if you are interested in the opportunity. If there is a quiet period during the interview, it might mean that the interviewer is contemplating or evaluating something you said or formulating her next question. You shouldn't feel pressured to break the silence. In fact, you may have heard from recruiters or interview coaches that the hiring authority may be testing you to see how you deal with silence. Although this may be true, it's a technique I choose not to employ, but some do. My advice to you is to be aware of an interviewer's intended silence and be comfortable during this time. You don't want to rush her into speaking just to bridge the gap. If you are unsure if the interviewer expected more information following a question, ask if she wanted to learn more from that last response.

Grammar 101

In an interview for an executive-level position, you should be able to articulate your thoughts with proper grammar. You don't want to sound stilted in your conversation, but you want to be sure of accurate word usage and pronunciation. Recently our firm presented a candidate who made it through to the third-round interview with the client company's CEO. In addition to leading his company, the CEO was an academic at a world-renowned think tank. When the candidate mispronounced a word during the interview with him, it was the classic nails-on-a-chalkboard irritant to the CEO. He ruled him out solely on that one error. Members of senior management who had moved him forward in the process were disappointed in their CEO's reaction, as the candidate was superlative in every other way, but they weren't surprised.

Recruiters and client executives expect you to be articulate and to avoid use of slang, profanity, and colloquialisms. Although you may use some industry jargon or buzzwords during the course of your interview, use them sparingly. And if your vocabulary is particularly broad, you'll want to ensure you don't appear to be talking down to the interviewer. Without dumbing down your vocabulary, the words you select should communicate clearly to the listener both your qualifications for the position and your command of the English language as a business communicator.

Have a Sense of Humor

When I meet a professional with a sense of humor, I know she will make a stronger impression in an interview situation than one who lacks that gift. A sense of humor conveys self-confidence and poise when employed appropriately. You've often heard that laughter is the best medicine. I've seen candidates walk into an interview and after a bit of small talk use humor to put people—and themselves—at ease. They command a certain presence and engage the interviewer with their wit and charisma. I'm sure you've been in a situation where a speaker trips going up to a podium or bungles a phrase. The speaker who handles the blunder with humor is seen as being in control and having grace. We're all human and all make mistakes. We forgive him and join the speaker in a heartfelt laugh over the incident. The blunderer who clamps her lips and glares at the audience pretending as if the incident never happened only looks foolish and ends up creating an embarrassing situation. If you can see the lighter side of a stressful situation, it can serve as a good antidote. You can ease tension in the workplace by not taking yourself so seriously. However, there are times when humor is inappropriate. When candidates are nervous during an interview, they might be tempted to say or do something inappropriate in hopes of getting a laugh. You don't want to burst into the room telling jokes or behave like a clown. Neither do you want to joke about weight, height, handicaps or other physical characteristics, age, race, ethnicity, gender or sexual preference, politics, or tragic circumstances. Staying away from jokes of that nature is common sense to many but not to all. Use your wit in an interview but not heavy-handed humor or jokes.

Think on Your Feet

We've all heard this expression. An executive should be able to think on his feet and respond intelligently and appropriately when asked a question or presented with a certain workplace issue or crisis and how to solve it. The reason this is so important is that it reveals that a candidate knows himself and has good judgment. Refer to the importance of knowing yourself in Chapter 8 on branding your career ("Candidate, Know Thyself") and judgment in Chapter 7 on the intangible qualities. You must at least possess good judgment to think on your feet in challenging situations or in a job interview. Years of experience and maturity also help you form an opinion or answer to certain questions posed or situations presented. By *thinking on your feet,* I don't necessarily mean being able to have a ready answer to a problem in a matter of seconds. However, you must know yourself well enough to respond that you don't know the answer or that you'd like more time to think about that rather than concocting a response that makes you look like you're frantically treading water.

Be Punctual and Courteous

Being punctual is critical in a job interview. You don't want to keep your prospective employer waiting. Not only does it display bad manners, but it also appears to convey disinterest in the job and a lack of respect for the executives' time. If you live outside the area, make plans to stay at a hotel closer to the interview site the day prior to the meeting to avoid traffic delays and airline cancellations. Why risk it? You only have one chance to make a good impression. Don't start an interview by rushing in flustered and making excuses why you were late. It shows you lack leadership presence. Work with the recruiter or the client company's scheduling contact to ensure that all arrangements are made and you know the directions to the interview site. I can't tell you how many times a candidate has expected a cab driver to know directions to a company's headquarters only to be met with a confused shake of the head.

Also, be courteous to all employees at the company. If you present yourself warmly and graciously to the hiring executives but are surly with the receptionist, you will not be invited back. You are working within an organization of people at all levels. Show your respect.

Perfumes/Colognes and Personal Grooming

As I discussed in the chapter on interviewing etiquette, avoid wearing strong perfumes or colognes when interviewing with the recruiter or the client executives. You want someone to remember you, not your perfume. In a business setting, fragrance can be distracting and offensive, particularly if someone is allergic to it. You don't want your fragrance to linger in an office long after you have left an interview. Strong fragrance should be reserved for personal, not business, use.

Meals and What to Order

Use your best judgment when ordering off a menu during meals hosted by a recruiter or a prospective employer. Your purpose in having a meal with these professionals is not for entertainment or a luxurious dining experience. The focus is the interview, not the meal. Order something that you can easily manage while talking and listening. Think about the message you send to the interviewers when you order a particular item. I'm sure you've heard that you shouldn't order something that you eat with your hands. Why? While holding the double cheeseburger with dripping sauce, you may be asked to show your samples, or someone else may join your party, and you'll need to either decline a handshake or first clean your sticky, greasy hand. You don't want to order something that is messy or takes a lot of time to prepare and eat. Just think for a moment about cracking open a lobster while someone asks you a question about your accomplishments in your company's Hong Kong division. You might need to ask her to repeat the question as you could not hear over the snapping of the crustacean's shell. And don't order food that is too hot, too spicy, or unfamiliar to you, or you might disrupt the interview with a coughing fit or embarrass yourself when the waiter presents you with a dish of raw turnips. On the other hand, if you are invited to a restaurant known for certain delicacies and your host suggests something that is the best in the world, you might think about ordering it. If you have particular dining restrictions, you should feel comfortable mentioning what they are up front so as not to appear finicky and reject every offering on the menu.

As for alcohol consumption during a meal, some recruiters recommend you stay away from alcohol during an interview, whereas others say a glass of wine is acceptable at dinner. This is a judgment call for you to make. If you feel you need a drink to get through the interview, you should abstain. If you are having dinner with the hiring executives and they encourage you to join them in a glass of wine, you should feel comfortable accepting. You know yourself and your limitations in this area. If you feel a glass of wine would impair your judgment, politely decline the offer. If a glass of wine is an occasional part of your dinner routine and you consume it slowly, it should not impact your performance during an interview. In some cultures it's perceived as rude not to accept a drink. Again, use your best judgment.

Who Controls the Interview?

You may not have given much thought as to who takes control of the interview agenda. You might have assumed it was the interviewer. In today's aggressive hiring market, the process has evolved to become more of an equal exchange between the interviewer and the candidate. The candidate is interviewing the hiring executive just as much as he is interviewing the candidate. This style has proven beneficial to both sides of the equation. Some client executives might bristle at the thought of the candidate taking control of the interview, as they might perceive the candidate as being overly aggressive or a micromanager. If you approach the perceived transfer of power appropriately, the interviewer will benefit from your proactive presentation and take the onus off him to pursue a presumably rote line of questioning. And if you assume a measured control of the interview, you won't walk away from it thinking, gee, the recruiter didn't ask me about the business unit I grew by 150 percent. It's possible that the executive didn't ask that question because he was tired or that part of your resume didn't pop out at the interviewer. If you manage the situation properly, you'll make sure your key points are delivered and at the same time demonstrate your leadership abilities.

The Conversational Interview

I've had candidates debrief with me following an interview with client executives only to come away feeling disappointed in themselves. When I ask why, they say the interviewer never asked any of the tough questions they were anticipating. As I mentioned earlier, today's interviewing style has changed dramatically from that of prior decades. It's much more of a two-way conversation than in the past. The goal of the interviewer is to learn as much as possible about your professional accomplishments and your core competencies in just a couple of hours. It's my opinion that much of what they need to know will be revealed in a dialogue more than in the stiff, traditional question-and-answer interview style. If you are a proactive interviewee, you will be certain to cover the topics and deliver the key messages you believe are imperative for the recruiter or hiring executive to know.

As I mentioned in prior chapters, I conduct an interview with a candidate by asking her to tell me about her professional background from the first job out of college to the present time. In this way, the professional typically interjects experiences that she believes are important, along with more personal information that an interviewer does not pointedly ask a candidate. The candidate usually becomes more comfortable and open during the conversation, and both the recruiter and the candidate benefit from the exchange. The recruiter gains knowledge about additional facets of the individual, and the candidate is able to demonstrate her intangible assets in this type of discussion.

However, not all executives conduct an interview in this dialogue style, and you need to be prepared to respond to the traditional command-and-control, let-me-fire-off-the-questions-and-you-answer style.

The Stress Interview

The stress interview is a technique employed more than two decades ago. Some executives prefer this confrontational interview style. If you have multiple interviews, perhaps someone in the group will be designated to conduct a stress interview. Typically this individual will come across as hostile and disinterested in you as a candidate. He may not pay attention to you or ask you questions that appear insulting or argumentative. The goal of the stress interview is to see how you handle pressure. It tests your poise. Will she maintain grace under fire? I've had candidates comment to me that they feel they have endured a stress interview with one of my client executives, and I've addressed it with the client as an issue. I don't believe there's much to be gained by employing this tactic. It only serves to fluster the candidate and you don't learn more about her than you would have in a more civilized exchange. Most candidates who suffer through this experience tell me they have no interest in working for a company because of the lack of respect and poor treatment shown by the executive. If you think you have encountered a stress interviewer, simply answer his questions and don't take the bait by engaging in a heated discussion. Similarly, you don't want to confront a recruiter or prospective employer in a hostile manner. You have nothing to gain by asking the interviewer anything that could be construed as being antagonistic.

Interviewing Before a Panel

Sometimes a client will prefer to conduct a panel interview with a group of executives and occasionally also subordinates of the position the company is seeking to fill. Depending on your dislike of group presentations in general, you may dread such an interview. It's understandable that you may not enjoy such a process. In a panel interview it can be difficult to know whom to address, and you may feel as though you are in the hot seat with so many key executives training their eyes on you. Do your best to relax. Make eye contact with each person, just as you would in a one-on-one interview. It might turn into a lively discussion. In preparation for the panel interview, ask the recruiter for a biographical sketch of each person involved so that you'll know your audience (and, by the way, you should review the biographies of all executives you meet in the one-on-one interview format as well!)

Honesty

"Honesty is the best policy" can't ring more true than in an interview situation. Be candid, direct, honest, and professional in your dealings with the executive search professional and with the prospective employer. Someone who lacks integrity and thinks he can fool the interviewer is sadly mistaken. We may not recognize a dishonest individual right away, but eventually he will be exposed. Discrepancies start showing up. As I mentioned in prior chapters, there will always be someone we know who knows you. Even stretching the truth on your resume is grounds for being blackballed in the executive search community. Don't do it. It's your career to ruin.

Do Your Homework!

Besides being caught lying, if you are perceived by the interviewer as not having conducted research on the company, you can assume that your interview will be cut short and you will not be invited back for another round. During the interview, the hiring executives will want to know what you know about their company and why you are interested in a position there. Perhaps you went into the interview with indifference and you didn't really read much about the company beyond a paragraph or two. Are you going to tell them that? No, unless you really are not interested, in which case you never should have taken your candidacy that far. But more than likely, if you have moved forward in the search process to the point of interviewing with the client company, you will have a strong level of intrigue, and you will want to respond intelligently to the executives' questions. So be prepared. Get copies of the company's annual report and 10K. Review the company's financials and business strategy and those of their competitors by using the World Wide Web. Become familiar with the CEO's vision and management style. Know where their regional offices, plants, and facilities are located. Understand some of the issues facing the company and its industry. Read recent newspaper and magazine articles on the company and get to know it's culture as much as possible. Review the biographical information of the people that will be interviewing you. It's up to you to conduct your due diligence.

Some candidates expect the recruiter to prepare them for an interview with the client executives. Although recruiters can and do provide the candidate with some materials on the company or refer them to its Web site or other such source, it is incumbent upon the candidate to take the initiative and conduct his own research. In preparing you for the interview, the search professional can offer suggestions on the client executives' management style and perhaps interviewing style and give you a broad-brush overview of the organization, but *you* must go beyond the surface prior to your meetings. And make a list of questions you'll want to ask the client executives, as the headhunter can only have so much information on the company and can't be expected to answer the in-depth questions you might have.

You'll also want to be sure you have reacquainted yourself with your own background and experience. I've asked candidates about a position they held five years ago, and they can't remember dates, names, events, or numbers that are relevant to the opportunity they are interested in. So much can happen in your career in a five-year period that information from a position you held at that time can fade from your memory. Don't expect yourself to be able to dredge up everything an interviewer will ask you from jobs gone by, but to prevent yourself from appearing less than bright and risk having the hiring executive question whether you had the experience you say you do, refresh your memory. Dig up your old annual reports or do some online historical research. If you can't remember your own career details, it can also make the interviewer (both hiring executive and recruiter) feel that perhaps you were not fully engaged and immersed in a particular position—a significant blow to your career navigation efforts! Practice interviewing with a colleague or mentor so that the information will be fresh in your mind, and your answers will be rehearsed. You don't want your responses to appear canned, but you will want to appear confident and that you can think on your feet. Remember: Candidate, know thyself!

The Top 21 Questions You Must Be Prepared to Answer

Even though you may experience interviews in the conversational style, you need to be prepared to answer the more conventional questions that interviewers typically ask. And even in a dialogue-style interview, you'll want to have answers to these questions at the ready as they will surface during the course of the conversation, they just might not be asked in the same manner.

1. *Tell Me About Yourself:* Start with your education and provide a chronological account of your work experience. Keep it brief and touch on the highlights of each position and company. Use this time to sell yourself to the company and focus on the points that make you a strong candidate for the position. Don't drone on or give too much detail. If the interviewer wants more in-depth information, she will ask. Plan on a 15- to 20-minute overview.

2. *What Are Your Key Accomplishments?* The interviewer wants to know what you *accomplished* in each position, not just your responsibilities. Plan to support your claims with facts and figures—for example, you grew a business unit by 75 percent, or your team's efforts increased revenues by 100 percent. If you established a function and were promoted

several times, mention these achievements as well. Be sure these accomplishments are recent, not from 10 years ago!

3. *What are Your Strengths and Weaknesses?* Give this a lot of thought before the interview. Your strengths are presumably simple for you to identify; your weaknesses probably are not. Without being self-deprecating, you should know one or two areas of potential improvement. If you say you have no weaknesses, you may be perceived as either a finger pointer or clueless.

4. *Reason for Leaving Each Position:* Be honest about why you left each job. Were you promoted? Fired? Recruited to a better opportunity? If your reason for leaving was that you did not agree with management's style or had problems with your last boss, you'll want to position this carefully so you don't appear to be a troublemaker. And if you were fired, explain why. Recruiters and hiring executives are familiar with many other companies' management and will likely know the situation.

5. *What's Your Management Style?* Be prepared to explain your management style and that of your company. In general, how do you get results? You should know if you are assertive, proactive, a good mentor, a leader by example, a team player, or a change agent.

6. *Why Are You Interested in This Position?* I've had candidates tell me they're in it for the money. This should not be your response. Even if it appears to be the primary reason for you, it actually goes deeper than that. It may be an opportunity to broaden your management capabilities, expand into a new industry, or manage a larger team. This typically also will result in higher compensation.

7. *How Do You Handle Stress/Criticism/Praise?* Cite examples for the interviewer as to how you handled a situation under stress and with praise. Perhaps

there were massive layoffs, or a manufacturing facility burned down. What was your role in these incidents, and how did you manage your own stress as well as that of others? Was there a situation where you were criticized for a problem you created or handled poorly? Again, we're all human and we all make mistakes. You don't want to say you were never criticized for anything. That would appear to be dishonest. The interviewer will want to know how you recovered from the issue. As for praise, you'll want to mention how you handled it graciously and cite examples of when you received such commendations from the company. It's an opportunity for you to shine.

8. *What Would Your Boss/Peers/Subordinates Say about You?* The interviewer will want to gauge your self-perception as well as what you perceive that others think of you. He also will want to gain a sense of your respect within an organization and if you are a team player. This question also provides you with an opening to discuss your outstanding achievements through your boss's or colleagues' eyes. Your response will allow you to reveal your strengths and accomplishments.

9. *Are You Looking at Other Opportunities?* If you are interviewing elsewhere, you should be honest about it. You don't need to mention the specific companies, but you should be forthcoming about where you might be in the overall recruitment process, as the company pursuing you might decide it is of value to complete its efforts to recruit you on a quicker timeline.

10. *Are You Willing to Relocate?* If you truly are interested in an opportunity, the answer to this question should be yes. And if you believe the position might mean relocating again, such as to a facility in another location or with significant time spent overseas, volunteer that you are flexible. Conversely, if you are unwilling to consider a specific position because future promotions within that organization

may mean a tour of duty overseas (or even moving to another city in the United States), be candid about this view as well.

11. *Where Do You See Yourself in 5 or 10 Years?* You should have a good sense of where you want to go in your career, but use your best judgment in responding. If your goal is to become CEO in 1 year and the CEO who is interviewing you doesn't have plans to leave the company for 5, it's best to not make that your goal, or you may be implying to her you plan to remain in the job for only a defined amount of time. Use common sense and state your goals. You might also ask the hiring executive about the career path for the position you are seeking.

12. *Why Should We Hire You?* You should be able to respond with self-confidence that you believe your qualifications and attributes make you an outstanding candidate for the position and give four or five reasons why. Don't just say because you are the best candidate for the job!

13. *What Would Be Your Perfect Job?* This is a ridiculous question, but answer it graciously, and if you believe the position you are interviewing for has certain aspects of a perfect job, cite the attractive points. If you describe a job that is nothing like the job for which you are interviewing, you probably won't be invited back for further interviews.

14. *Tell Me about the Best/Worst Decision You Made:* The interviewer will want to know about your judgment abilities, as I discussed in Chapter 7. And although you may have made a bad judgment call, the most important part of that is how you recovered from it and what you learned from it. As for your best decision, support your assertion with results, facts, and figures.

15. *What Obstacles Prevented You from Achieving Your Goals in Your Current/Last Job?* Answer this one cautiously. You want to be honest with the interviewer, but if it was because your boss did not respect you or

you were unable to meet the company's projected financial goals, you will need to position your answer carefully and properly.

16. *What Motivates You and How Do You Motivate Others?* You probably don't want to say "money"! However, again, be honest as to what your passions are. What makes you want to get up and go to work in the morning? What challenges you? What drives you? If you have trouble with this one, review the intangible qualities I discussed in Chapter 7 to gain a better overall understanding of what inspires you to take action and what you do to cascade your message through your organization.

17. *Describe the Culture at Your Current/Past Company:* You should have a good understanding of the company's culture and how to articulate it. Or you might say that as a start-up its culture is evolving or is fast paced and so on. The interviewer will want to know if you are comfortable in that culture. If your company's culture is the same as that of the company at which you are interviewing and you don't like the culture, it doesn't make sense to pursue the opportunity.

18. *Tell Me More about Your Current/Past Company and Its Competitors:* Be prepared to give a capsule of the company's financials, its business plan, management style, background on key executives, growth strategy, deficiencies, CEO vision, industry trends, and so on. You should also be able to cite the same for two or three of its competitors. You want to ensure you are viewed as a credible expert in your industry and functional discipline.

19. *What Do You Know about Our Company?* If you have done your homework as I discussed in earlier pages, you can cite company facts. But beyond that, you want to discuss what is appealing about the company and why you are interested in an opportunity there. If you inquire as to a particular issue at the company—its business plan, class-action lawsuit, or

pending merger—don't put the executive on the defensive. Ask about their strategy in addressing these issues or praise them for their quick response to a problem. You won't score any points with the company's executives if you are overly critical of their approach.

20. *What Are Your Interests outside of Your Career?* "All work and no play ..." and you know the rest. A prospective employer wants to know what your passions are other than work. You don't want to say you have none. You're not a robot, after all. Share some of your outside interests and experiences with your interviewer. Do you enjoy mountain biking? sailing? volunteer work at the local hospital or animal shelter? raising five kids? Maybe you enjoy collecting something. You probably don't want to make it appear as though your avocation absorbs too much of your time, but you want to show that you are a well-adjusted, well-rounded professional. And, it will help the interviewer determine whether you are a good cultural fit with the organization.

21. *What Books Have You Read Recently?* It seems that every interviewer asks this question of candidates. In addition to getting a better idea of your interests, knowing what books you read tells the interviewer that you are continually self-educating and possess intellectual curiosity. Maybe the books you read support your quest for knowledge in business or your particular industry or area of focus. Or what you choose to read may take you far away from your day-to-day responsibilities. You might enjoy suspense novels or sports biographies. It's okay to say that you haven't read a book lately. Perhaps you prefer reading business magazines. Whatever the realities are, be prepared to answer this question without looking foolish. And don't say you've read something if you haven't! The interviewer may want to share some thoughts with you about his favorite passage or dis-

cuss the story line with you, and if you indeed know nothing about it, you've created a rather serious dilemma for yourself!

Questions the Interviewer Can't Ask

There are federal and state laws that govern what a prospective employer or recruiter can ask you in a job interview. For example, in California it is illegal to ask a candidate if you own your own home, how old you are, where were you born, and if you are married. Now, you might volunteer answers to those questions before the interviewer asks them, and that's not illegal. However, it's to your benefit to be as open and honest as possible with both the recruiter and the hiring executive, particularly when you receive an offer and get down to negotiating compensation. At this point in time, owning your home or relocating a family becomes important information to share. If you believe sharing this information will eliminate you as a candidate for an opportunity, you probably wouldn't want to pursue employment with a company that you believe may endorse discriminatory practices anyway. Remember, very few organizations are seeking this information for negative reasons. A company's or recruiter's sole intent should be to gain as much knowledge about you professionally and personally (in essence, they want to know the whole person) so as to create the best match and a successful opportunity for you.

The 10 Most Common Questions You Should Ask

A strong candidate will be expected to ask strategic questions during the course of a job interview, whether it is with the recruiter or the prospective employer. Often the interviewer will ask at the end or sometimes at the beginning of the meeting if you have any questions. You should be pre-pared with a list of thoughtful questions to ask. It's not the quantity of questions that count, it's how insightful your ques-tions are and the level of understanding of the position and the company's goals that your questions demonstrate. In ask-ing your questions, you want to be certain they have not already been addressed in the company's annual report or other materials, as this will reveal that you did not conduct thorough research on the company prior to your interview. That will not bode well with the hiring executive, and she is likely to take a dim view of your lack of preparatory work. If many of your questions have been answered during the course of the interview, mention that. Don't just say "No, I don't have any." Your queries will also demonstrate your inter-est in the opportunity and the company. And as I mentioned earlier, you don't want to put your interviewer on the defen-sive in your line of questioning, but if you have a particular concern with a company's strategy or direction, address that issue in a forthright manner. Perhaps in the 10K there was a mention of a pending merger. This would certainly arouse a candidate's curiosity as, depending upon the type of position he is seeking, completion of the merger may eliminate the position for which the candidate is interviewing. The types of questions you want to consider asking include the following:

1. What are the immediate and long-term goals of the position?
2. What is the career path for this position?
3. In what ways do you see this position supporting the company's strategic goals and objectives?
4. How does your company measure performance?
5. Why did the person before me fail in this role (if that was the case)?
6. How would you describe the company's culture? What are the strengths of the operating culture? What are the areas of the company's culture that the senior management team would like to improve (if applicable)?

7. Can you tell me more about the company's plans for growth in the next three to five years?

8. Can you tell me more about the management style of the people with whom I would be working?

9. What do you see as the company's competitive advantages?

10. Is there anything else I can tell you about my background and experience to give you more insight into my qualifications for the position?

Presumably you will not need to ask all of these questions, and you will likely formulate others you'll want to ask. These questions are intended as guidelines. You'll want to be certain that you have as much information possible about the position and the company to shape your decision if an offer is extended to you. Other questions regarding such issues as employee benefits and compensation should be addressed in subsequent interviews once you become the finalist candidate.

A Word on Cultural Fit

Suppose you have made the rounds of interviews with the recruiter and he is delighted with your candidacy and presents you as a semifinalist on the panel. The client wants to meet with you. You interview with three client executives, and you feel all went very well. The recruiter calls to tell you that you are one of two candidates selected to return to meet with the CEO and other members of senior management. By this time you feel pretty confident that you are the one who is likely to get the job offer, as you feel you've made a strong case for your candidacy. You meet the CEO and the other executives and feel you've scored very high during the interview. Your spouse is excited about the prospect of moving to a new community and has spent time on the Internet looking at new homes. You've given your references to the recruiter and fully anticipate the offer in a day or two. You can't wait for the phone call. The recruiter calls and tells you that an offer was made to the other candidate. You can hardly believe it! What could you have possibly done wrong? Your spouse asks you how you could have blown this opportunity of a lifetime. A recruiter who has integrity will tell you why you did not get the offer. Sometimes it's just that the other candidate was a better cultural fit. What exactly does that mean? It means that you had the technical skills and appeared to be a good fit within the organization, but the other professional was a stronger overall fit. *Cultural fit* is not easy to define. It's something that the hiring executives will base primarily on gut feel. However, there are some guideposts upon which to base that assessment beyond instinct, such as corporate values, management style, operational behaviors, attitude toward change, progressive or conservative nature, diversity, organizational structure of your company, and so on. Someone who has more of an entrepreneurial nature will not be comfortable in a command-and-control culture. You shouldn't take offense at being the runner up based on lack of cultural fit. Seek an opportunity where the culture is one in which you will flourish and have the opportunity to meet or exceed your own intended career goals.

Secret: Abracadabra, hocus-pocus, mumbo jumbo—oh, okay, open sesame, too! Let's get real—there is *no such thing* as magic in the interview process. So take a deep breath. Put away the magic wand, the smoke and the mirrors, and just be real and be yourself. That's all it takes!

CHAPTER 10

The Secrets of Negotiating Compensation

Whether you are seeking a new position in a different company or accepting a new role within your current organization, the secret to negotiating your compensation starts with evaluating your annual worth. You need to determine your marketplace value to give yourself the additional, valuable criteria to leverage when negotiating your new compensation package. After all, you might be faced with a human resource professional who is not current with the changing marketplace and may not know all the elements involved in presenting you with an attractive offer. As a result, *you* need to make it your job to know all of your options.

How Do You Calculate Your Marketplace Value?

In today's corporate America, calculating your marketplace value can be one of the more difficult assignments in your job search. Is your marketplace value equal to your current total compensation package? Is it 20 percent above that? If you move from the Midwest to New York City or Silicon Valley, does your marketplace value increase, decrease, or stay the same? If you are not employed by a technology company, is your marketplace value lower?

These are all valid questions and can be difficult for you, the candidate, to answer when sitting down with a recruiter, prospective employer, or your current company's senior management. In prior years, determining marketplace value was a simpler process, with traditional corporate America looking at candidates fresh out of college aiming to remain with the company until retirement. There were just not as many variables to consider then as now. The dot-com companies that emerged in the 1990s, although many died a quick death, have put executive compensation packages wildly out of focus. The rules of the new economy continue to change daily. Where do you begin in calculating your marketplace value?

The Compensation Components That Make Up Your Annual Worth

The Compensation Evolution chart (Table 10.1) that I designed illustrates the components that are critical for you to determine in order to maximize your current annual worth and leverage in calculating your value as a candidate when negotiating a new compensation package (whether the opportunity is with a new company or it's annual review time at your current employer). You'd be surprised how many candidates I interview who have no idea what their current annual worth is as an employee. When I ask candidates if they know their current compensation, they typically give me base salary, bonus, and stock options. When I inquire about their other perks or benefits, usually a light goes on, and they might mention participation in health care and 401(k) programs. Okay. Now, what are some of the other hidden benefits? By *hidden benefits*, I mean those components you might not always take into consideration when determining your annual compensation, such as company car, travel awards, health care or day care facilities, work-at-home programs, and others. The light gets brighter. Oh, they say, I hadn't thought about those things as part of my compensation!

Take a look at Table 10.1, find your career/position level, and examine all the variables. While doing so, I'd like you to make a list of your components and determine your current overall compensation and marketplace value. (Note that not all of these components will apply to your level.) It is critical to your career navigation to have this information in your files when the recruiter calls or when you receive a job offer or promotion to maximize your negotiating power. And be sure to update these benchmark criteria every time the components change and also when your job responsibilities broaden, as this also affects your marketplace value. Later in the chapter I'll discuss how to negotiate these components.

In my opinion, all professionals should have a directory in their *home* computer (note that I did not indicate your computer at work) that is all about them and their professional life. Some of the contents of this directory would include your resume, a list of current references, and a chart focusing exclusively on compensation. In the chart, you should have three distinct columns with the following headings: current compensation, compensation if relocating to a higher cost-of-living market, and compensation if changing jobs within the same geographic region where you presently reside. The following sections of this chapter will address each of the line-item categories with which you should become familiar and be comfortable articulating in any

Table 10.1 TRRG, Inc. Compensation Evolution

	Manager Level and Below	Director
I. Primary Compensation Elements		
Base salary	√	√
Target annual bonus eligibility	√	√
Stock options	N/A	√*
Sign-on bonus	N/A	√*
Title	Confirm it	Confirm it
Early performance/ review dates	Depends on what is negotiated for the first year of employment	Depends on what is negotiated for the first year of employment
Company car	N/A	N/A
Executive tax preparation	N/A	N/A
Executive annual physical	N/A	N/A
II. Relocation Benefits		
Relocation assistance		
• Monetary	N/A	Depends on the company policy
• Home selling/ buying assistance	N/A	N/A
• Transportation of household goods	Yes, in most cases	√
• House hunting trip	Depends on the company policy	√
• Temporary housing	N/A	Negotiable
III. Miscellaneous Benefits		
Health care benefits		
• Medical and dental	√	√
• Life insurance	N/A	N/A
Profit-sharing/401(k)/ retirement programs	√	√
Spousal career assistance	N/A	N/A
Vacation	√	√
Use of technology	N/A	√
Training/education	Amount depends on company policy	Amount depends on company policy
Travel awards	Amount depends on company policy	Amount depends on company policy

Vice President	Senior Vice President	Executive Vice President and Higher
√	√	√
√	√	√
√	√	√
√	√	√
Confirm it	Confirm it	Confirm it
Depends on what is negotiated for the first year of employment	Depends on what is negotiated for the first year of employment	Depends on what is negotiated for the first year of employment
√*	√	√
Depends on the company policy	√	√
Depends on the company policy	√	√
Depends on the company policy	Depends on the company policy	Depends on the company policy
Sometimes	√	√
√	√	√
√	√	√
√	√	√
√	√	√
√	√**	√**
√	√	√
Sometimes applicable	√	√
√	√	√
√	√	√
Amount depends on company policy	Amount depends on company policy	Amount depends on company policy
Amount depends on company policy	Amount depends on company policy; however, there may be special programs at this level	Amount depends on company policy; however, there may be special programs at this level

*May not apply at some companies.   **Funded by employer in most cases.

compensation conversation, whether it is with a recruiter, the hiring executive, or your current boss.

Primary Compensation Elements

Base Salary

Determining your base salary is simple if you are a salaried and not a commissioned employee or an independent consultant. I'm sure most, if not all, of you reading this know that your base salary is your annual pretax earnings paid by your employer. It does not include any bonuses, perks, or other forms of remuneration.

Target Annual Bonus Eligibility

Your target annual bonus eligibility is typically a combination of elements—your individual performance, your team's performance, your business unit's performance, and the company's performance. Some bonuses are based solely on the employee's performance in meeting certain predetermined individual goals, but most are contingent upon other, broader targets being met. Depending upon what base salary you negotiated in your current job, you might find that your annual performance bonus could be 20 to 30 percent of your base, or it could be 100 percent of your base or more. You may have seen CEOs take one dollar in annual base salary and significant bonus eligibility. If the company does well, their annual bonus could net them millions of dollars. Sometimes a bonus is guaranteed, sometimes not. Be sure you mention this qualifier when discussing your annual bonus eligibility.

Stock Options

Over the past several years, particularly in the new economy, stock option plans have become a tremendously important and highly lucrative component of an executive's compensation package. A recent article in *Working Woman* magazine touted a 1999 study conducted of 350 large U.S. corporations by William M. Mercer that found that approximately 39 percent now have broad-based stock option plans covering more than half of all employees. In 1993, only 17 percent offered options. Stock option plans vary from company to company, and there may be more than one type of program for different executives operating simultaneously. Sometimes employees at the managerial level can participate in the stock option plan; at other companies participation in the program is offered only at the higher ranks. Whoever is allocated stock options needs to be approved by the company's board of directors. If you are eligible to participate in a stock option program, what is your particular plan? Most often a typical plan involves options that are allocated to you when you join the company, and you have the option to buy them in the future at the "strike price," or market price at which the company's shares traded the day you joined the company. (Sometimes the strike price can be determined by the company, depending upon the rank of the executive and the stock option program in which she is eligible to participate.) These options vest over a period of time, let's say four or five years and at 20 or 25 percent each year. Some programs offer monthly vesting spread out equally over the four- or five-year period.

Other stock option programs include restricted stock grants. In this program, the company *gives* you shares in the company, usually for meeting certain performance goals or as a long-term incentive. Often to exercise these grants a goal must be met within a certain period of time. Let's say you have a 10,000-share grant that vests at a rate of 2,500 shares every year over a four-year period. You'll need to remain with the company for four years to receive the entire grant. Some companies offer phantom stock options, grants that give the employee the right to receive the difference in market value between the share price at the time she received them and a time in the future that she chooses (could be several years) after an initial waiting period. Stock purchase plans allow employees to purchase a limited amount of stock at a price less than the market price to the public or purchase it at market price and the company will match dollar-for-dollar or at a specified cent-on-the-dollar rate.

Optimally, the market price of the company's stock will be higher when you become vested. However, if your strike price is higher than the market price at vesting time, the value of your stocks will be "under water," meaning they are essentially worth nothing until the market price rises above the strike price. If you are a participant in a stock option program, you understand that the value of stock options is a moving target, so when you are determining stock option value as part of your overall marketplace worth, you understand that their value fluctuates. If you are unsure what your stock option program involves or how to calculate the value of your options, speak to your stock plan administrator within your company.

Sign-On Bonus

When you joined your current company, did you receive a sign-on bonus? You should not expect to receive a sign-on bonus with every new job offer, but in today's job market many candidates do. A sign-on bonus is used to attract a candidate to make up for joining the company due to timing that prevents her from immediate participation in certain other executive incentive programs, to counter bonuses left behind at her other job, or to just sweeten the offer to a particularly stellar candidate. Other uses of a sign-on bonus might be to augment a relocation package or to make up for a slightly-lower-than-anticipated base salary in conjunction with an earlier performance review at the former company. Sign-on bonuses are usually paid in one lump sum at the onset of employment or in installments during the first six months to one year of employment. However, if you depart the company within one year after receipt, you could be asked to repay the company a partial amount. Sometimes a sign-on bonus will be paid in stock options as well. Remember, all of these details should be outlined in your offer letter.

Title and Reporting Relationship

Candidates may not think of their title when determining their overall marketplace value. Although titles mean something different in every company—for example, a vice president at a financial institution might be equivalent to a manager in a Fortune 100 company—some standards of recognition will apply to the meaning of your title. You might be head of a business unit responsible for managing a $200 million piece of the company and lead an organization of 500. And in today's world of creative titles, you might be called a team leader, chief knowledge officer, or in the case of Bill Gates, chief software architect. Similarly, in some high-technology companies you can hold the manager title even if you are being compensated for and have the same management responsibilities of a senior vice president in another organization. Recruiters and hiring authorities will consider your title and what accountability you have when determining your seniority. You'll also want to take into account to whom you report. If your title is manager or director and you report directly to the CEO, this presumably means you are of a higher rank than someone who reports to a less-senior executive in the organization. Title is difficult to quantify in dollars and cents, but it can be a good negotiating point. Most importantly, remember that it is not always about title—more germane to building your career brand and career momentum is the definition of the position, breadth of responsibilities, and overall upside potential of the job.

Early Performance Review

If you are eligible for an early performance review, that means you have the potential of a salary increase or an increase in other compensation components sooner than would be possible if you had to wait for an annual review. This is typically negotiated and given in the first year of employment. Include this when computing your compensation. When negotiating your new offer, mention the timing of your performance review, as your anticipated increase can be a factor in determining your new value.

Company Car

The value of your company car is what the company pays for the lease and any expenses paid in conjunction with it. Sometimes you are paid a monthly or annual allowance in lieu of the company picking up the lease payments. You may have opted for this choice if you prefer a different model than what the parameters of the lease provides, or you may have your own car and be happy with it. Whatever the arrangement, remember to include the value of this perk—after all, the IRS will!

Executive Tax Preparation

Tax preparation and general accounting services may be offered to executives and paid for by the company, generally at the vice presidential level and above. This service usually is offered to employees of larger companies. Depending upon your individual needs, the value of this program could be in the thousands of dollars annually.

Executive Annual Physical

Paying for an executive's annual physical not only benefits the employee but also the company, as it is in the best interest of the company to have healthy leaders! Even though physical exams are paid by many health care plans, it's a plus to have this benefit as a paid perk. Your human resources program administrators will be able to tell you the value of the physical if you are unsure of its worth.

Relocation Benefits

The next section of Table 10.1 deals with relocation benefits. When you accepted your most recent position, did you move to another city or state or perhaps to another country? If so, your compensation package most likely included relocation assistance. When calculating your marketplace value, you should include this as part of your overall compensation, and if offered a new position that requires relocation, you should be prepared to request it if it is not part of the offer. Even if it *is* offered, writing down all of the elements will better position you to negotiate. Relocation benefits may have been paid to you as a lump sum of cash to spend as you desired. Or you may have had assistance in selling your home, either through company-paid realtor fees or the company purchasing your home outright. You may also have had assistance in buying a home in the new location. This might have covered escrow costs, loan fees, and realtor fees. Other benefits might have included temporary housing, perhaps for two or three months; house-hunting trips to the new city; and, of course, the transportation of your household goods. The components of relocation benefits can be structured in any number of ways to best suit the needs and determined by the level of the candidate. How does the relocation package in the new offer stack up against your prior program?

Miscellaneous Benefits

Health Care Benefits

It's pretty simple to calculate the value of your health care benefits, as your company's benefits department should have provided you with all the information on your programs when you joined the company or became eligible to participate in health care benefits programs. Depending upon the executive's level, you might be looking at company-funded medical, dental, and life insurance premiums. Or your company might pay a portion of your medical and dental, and you pay the balance. Life insurance might be offered, or it might not. And if your employment is terminated (by you or the employer), did you know that it is standard policy at all corporations to offer you extended participation in a health care program, such as the Consolidated Omnibus Budget Reconciliation Act (COBRA) of 1985, which permits former employees to continue coverage for 18 months? That has value as well. If your benefits programs include domestic partner, elder care, and paternity programs, those components also have additional value.

Profit-Sharing/401(k)/Retirement Programs

Here again, the value of these programs should have been spelled out to you when you joined the company or became eligible for participation. Profit-sharing programs vary widely from company to company. Some might involve the company contributing a percentage of profits, whereas in others employees contribute a percentage and the company matches it dollar-for-dollar or a percentage. Similarly, 401(k) programs vary, typically with the employee becoming eligible for participation after a period of time employed, and can contribute a capped percentage of salary into the plan with the company matching 50 cents (or less) on the dollar up to a certain percentage. There are limits to what you can withdraw and at what age you can withdraw it without incurring high penalties. You should note the value of your program and what you might give up if you leave your position prior to the vesting period. Also remember that every company's retirement program will have different rules governing the plan, so be sure to understand your plan thoroughly—it is to your advantage.

Spousal Career Assistance

At the more senior executive level, the company will assist the trailing spouse in finding a position in the new city to which he or she relocated with the newly placed executive. Although value of this service might be difficult to quantify, it should be viewed as another component of your compensation. These programs vary from company to company but might involve paying for lost wages or benefits of the trailing spouse or covering job-hunting costs, counseling, and other such assistance.

Vacation

Vacation programs or time off might include your typical two-to four-week programs, but today there are many creative ways that companies compensate employees for time outside the office. Your plan may include a period of time off that can be used for sick time, personal days, or vacation days. Other programs could include extended time off during maternity leave, for the mother or father, and sabbaticals to learn new skills or travel the world in conjunction with a corporate program. Factor in any unique programs in which you are involved at your company. You won't necessarily have a dollars-and-cents figure in the column, but you still need to thoroughly understand your company's plan and that of a prospective employer.

Use of Technology

If you work for a technology company, you might believe that a laptop, cell phone, pager, personal digital assistant (PDA), fax machine, or other communications device for your personal use at home and while traveling are perks at every company. Not so. These electronics are categorized as another benefit and so have value in calculating your current compensation. If you had to replace every piece of electronic equipment your company either has provided you or pays for your use, it would total into the multiple thousands of dollars annually. Make a list of each item your company currently pays for and include that total in your marketplace value calculation. This component can be a valuable negotiating tool.

Training/Education

Your company may have helped finance tuition for your MBA or perhaps an undergraduate degree for you or your family members. Tuition assistance programs paid by your company might be another component of your compensation. In addition to including college tuition assistance in your calculations, don't forget professional educational seminars and retreats. Even though these programs add value to you as a company employee, the cost of these programs (which would have come out of your pocket) and the fact that having completed them makes you a more marketable candidate have tremendous value.

Travel Awards/Airline Clubs

All those miles you travel for business are likely to earn you thousands of frequent-flier miles annually. Does your company allow you personal use of them, or does it recycle them for executives' travel? These frequent-flier miles can oftentimes provide you and your family a nicer perk when it comes time to make vacation plans. And although this is a nonnegotiable perk, the general rule to follow is to simply be aware of how the programs work! In addition, you should also know whether or not airline clubs' memberships are reimbursable. These programs are worth hundreds of dollars annually.

Other Criteria

The components I've mentioned thus far are some of the more tangible elements of your overall compensation and are typical of a senior-level executive's package. There are other criteria you should consider in calculating your own marketplace value, such as the following:

- *Career track record:* If you have changed jobs every few years and zigzagged up the ladder in different industries or functions rather than staying in one job for 10 years or more, you will be perceived as having higher marketplace value.

- *Increase in assignments and responsibilities:* Although your title might not have changed over the past few years, you may have been given more responsibilities in your current role, or you might have served in an assignment overseas or in another department.

- *Size of company or department:* The company for which you work as well as your department may have grown significantly during your tenure, or your current company may be larger than the one you are considering for a new position.

- *Specialist versus generalist:* Depending upon the needs of the company, you might position yourself as having more intrinsic value as a specialist or as a generalist.

- *MBA, Ph.D., certification programs:* Higher education typically gives you higher marketplace value.

- *On-site company perks:* Your current company may have on its premises a fitness facility, day care center, dry cleaners, and meals offered free or at a substantially reduced cost.

- *Club memberships:* Include in your calculations the value of any business, athletic, or country club dues.

- *Work-at-home time:* Although this may be difficult to quantify, time spent working from home eliminates commuting time and expense and enables you more flexibility to care for children or aging parents or just time spent in your own space.

- *Geographic location:* The cost of living varies widely from city to city. You might need to make 30 percent or more than your base salary in your present company because of the higher cost of living in the city where the new position might be located. This is a critical factor to include in compensation negotiation discussions. Be wary of online tools to determine your cost of living. Although some may provide you with general guidelines, consult with a relocation expert or realtor for the most accurate cost-of-living differential.

Bring out your calculator, add up all of these components on your list, and you should have an approximate idea of your current compensation and marketplace value. If you feel you are missing something in your computation, tap into additional resources to help you calculate your worth, such as your mentors, peers, industry associations, insurance agents, realtors, and your favorite headhunter!

Negotiating the Actual Compensation Package—Guerrilla Warfare or Minute Waltz?

Now that you have determined your current marketplace value, let's take a look at the offer you may now have on the table. The optimal job offer will have the potential for both wealth creation and well-being—that is, your next career step should give you an opportunity to increase your overall compensation while providing you with balance in your life. If it doesn't, how do you approach the hiring executive and what do you say? When do you say it? How hard do you push? Which components are negotiable, and which are not? If you've never participated in compensation negotiation discussions, the prospect of wielding your own sword may seem a bit daunting.

However, negotiating your new compensation package is not as treacherous as it may seem, as long as you are realistic. You don't want to appear egotistical and ask for the moon, and neither do you want to be passive and expect the perfect package to be dropped in your lap. The secret is to take an active role in managing the negotiating process and work closely with the recruiter, the human resource executive, the CEO, or whomever is involved in this critical final step in your job search process. My secret to negotiating a compensation package between my client company and finalist candidate basically involves the following three steps:

Step One: The Candidate's Current Compensation

I determine the candidate's current marketplace value based on the components I've outlined in Table 10.1.

Step Two: The Candidate's Wish List

Once the candidate has provided me with her current, and detailed, compensation list, my strategy is to ask for her compensation expectations—or as I like to call it, a wish list. Your wish list is not something you should dash off quickly or compile based on what one colleague receives or an article on compensation trends. You can visit Web sites, poll executive recruiters, study salary surveys, talk to other professionals in your industry or area of specialization, and contact colleagues and members of professional associations. Conduct extensive research and ask these individuals what someone with your educational experience, professional qualifications, and achievements is most likely to command and match this against your marketplace value. Take a hard look at yourself and compare what you bring to the table—including your proven career track record and the intangible assets I discussed in Chapter 7.

Now, armed with all of this information, I engage my candidate in a very candid dialogue about her wish list, dividing it into three categories:

1. The elements of the compensation package with which my client, or her prospective employer, will have no problems.

2. The compensation elements which I feel are highly negotiable and with which I believe the client may have flexibility—components that might tip the scale to work to both parties' advantage.
3. The candidate's expectations with which I believe the client will not agree.

Your secret to negotiating successfully lies within the second category. If you push hard in categories one or three, you risk losing the offer. Here's how I manage the dance.

Step Three: Counseling the Client and the Hiring Executive

One of the most critical roles that I can serve as a headhunter is to assist the hiring executive in navigating this final and critical part of the search process. In this step, I will take all the information I compiled on the candidate—the compensation components/marketplace value and the wish list, combined with any and all insights into the candidate's mind-set about compensation expectations, hot buttons, limitations, and other extenuating factors—and counsel my client as effectively as possible. In addition, I believe it is my responsibility as the recruiter to have deep and broad knowledge about relevant issues tied to a specific profession or function so that I can also impart that wisdom to both the client and the candidate as I advise them. Given the unique circumstances and factors of each situation, it is my goal that neither the client nor the candidate endure lengthy negotiations. Will it be guerrilla warfare or the minute waltz? If the sun, the moon, and all the planets align, I will have brought both the client and the candidate to a successful conclusion. How do I define *successful conclusion*? Both the client executive and the candidate should feel as though they each came out a winner at the end of the negotiation process, which is often the prickliest part of the entire search process.

The Negotiable Elements—Q & A

How do you determine which elements are negotiable? The best way for you to figure this out is to look at your list of compensation components and come up with your wish list. Where are *you* willing to be flexible? If you feel your ultimate goal is to hold the title of vice president or CEO and there is just no way you would give that up, you have to be prepared to reject the offer if it doesn't include the title you want. It might not be a negotiating point for the client company. If you have a strong interest in the opportunity and push too hard on this point, the client executives might rescind the offer. Negotiating the offer is a very delicate balancing act—one in which respected executive recruiters have experience.

Let me answer some of the questions I anticipate you'll have during this final phase of the search process and clear up some of the mysteries and myths of the negotiation dance.

Should I negotiate even if I'm happy with an offer?

No. If you believe the prospective employer has offered you everything or nearly everything on your wish list, why negotiate? Is it because your Uncle Fred told you to always go back for more? Some companies will present their best offer up front, and if it meets your expectations, why risk losing the offer or irritating your next employer? Do you want to appear as though you behaved in one manner during the interview process, and when it came time to negotiate the offer you turned into a madman or (-woman)? If you are happy with the offer, accept it. If not, be diplomatic in your negotiations.

They say your next job should give you an increase in base salary of 20 percent. If I'm offered less than that, should I try to negotiate it higher?

I don't know who "they" are who came up with that percentage. If you feel comfortable using a 20 percent increase as a general target increase on base salary for your next career step, then do so. However, you need to take into consideration all of the compensation components offered to you before setting your sights on an arbitrary 20 percent increase over your current base salary. It might turn out that a 20 percent increase is actually lower than what your marketplace value dictates or higher than what the current job market will bear. Or, once the complete compensation package is divulged, there may be other elements beyond the salary that warrant a lower annual base. Bottom line: be open-minded and flexible.

Where do you feel the most negotiating flexibility might be in the package?

In my experience, annual bonus eligibility, stock options, and the sign-on bonus offer the most flexibility across the greatest number of levels of positions/seniority in a company. You might find higher stock options more attractive than a higher base salary because of the long-term upside potential of the options based on the goals and objectives of the company. You may be a first-time home owner, and the relocation assistance program in your offer includes help with buying a home. As a new parent, more time to work at home or vacation time could be more appealing to you. Or you may be at a point in your career where an M.B.A. will help launch you into the next level of management, and the offer includes an attractive tuition assistance program.

I believe one of the most flexible and attractive components is the sign-on bonus. It's a wonderful recruitment tool
that's not used often enough, yet it is a simple answer to what
otherwise would result in losing a top candidate. The signing
bonus allows the candidate to get the financial compensation
in one year that he feels is deserved. It also gives the hiring
authority the opportunity to measure the added value the new
hire brings to the company. If the professional exceeds expectations, he might receive a significant jump in base salary in
a year or two. For example, suppose that the base salary range
for a position is $140,000 to $150,000 annually, an attractive
candidate is currently earning $150,000, and the salary on her
wish list is $175,000. The company wants to hire this indi-
vidual and doesn't want to risk losing her based on offering a
lower-than-acceptable salary. However, the company's human
resource department needs to maintain its peer equity, and
the $175,000 would disrupt the employee ecosystem, other-
wise defined as a salary administration plan. Hence, a signing bonus of $25,000 becomes a recruiting tool for solving the
impasse, and it is a win-win situation for both the candidate
and hiring executive.

Do I tell Company A that's just offered me a job that I have an offer from Company B?

Understandably, if you are interested in going to work for Company A, you would not want to risk losing the offer from that
company only to find that Company B has moved on to the
next candidate because you took too long to make a decision.
However, you should be honest about looking at other opportunities. Most prospective employers expect top-notch candidates to have multiple offers in today's hiring market. You don't
need to go into great detail about the offer or name the other
company, but you should let Company A know you are in talks
with Company B and have a responsibility to respond to B in

x period of time. Whatever your decision, be sure to respond to both companies in a reasonable period of time.

How long do I have to give the prospective employer an answer?

There is no hard and fast rule to the appropriate time frame for responding to an offer. You need to use your own best judgment and that of the executive recruiter. If the hiring authority wants your answer the next day and that won't work for you, be diplomatic in telling him the reason why you cannot respond that quickly. You are allowed to sleep on it. You might position with the prospective employer that you need some time to respond because it is a very important decision—particularly if it involves moving 3,000 miles across the country—and you need two days to discuss it with your family and then make your decision. The hiring executives should respect the timing of your decision-making process. If you have an interview in a couple of weeks with Company B and tell the company you'll get back to them at that time, Company A might not be amenable to this option. If there's an equally strong finalist candidate, they're very likely to forgo you as a candidate, as perhaps you aren't as enthusiastic about the opportunity as they thought. Timing is critical. And you need to be cognizant of the company's patience threshold. Some companies won't get into a bidding war with other companies over candidates. You stand to lose both offers if you don't exercise caution in pitting one company against another.

Doesn't the headhunter represent the client company? Why would she negotiate in my favor?

Even though a retained executive recruiter is compensated by the client company, she wants to arrive at a successful conclusion for both candidate and client; the offer should satisfy the goals of both parties. It is in the best interest of the search professional to assist in negotiating a fair and equitable package for the candidate because it's all about building long-term relationships. Reputable recruiters will actively negotiate on your behalf as well as the client.

What if I need "X" amount because of my kid's college tuition, my mortgage, and vacation home remodel?

Don't negotiate based on need. The prospective employer doesn't care what you need to pay your bills. A new employer cares about your marketplace value, how it might compare with the value the company puts on the position, and how it fits into the salary administration plan.

What about employment contracts, severance packages, change-in-control clauses, and noncompete agreements? How do I negotiate those?

Some of these guaranteed employment contracts and covenants are reserved only for the senior most executives. However, in business law, a verbal contract is just as enforceable as a written one, but there are limitations to what a verbal agreement can do for you. You need to verify your state's laws regarding such contracts. Most employers today will give you an offer letter, or letter of agreement, outlining the basics, such as base salary, bonus eligibility, stock option plan, vacation time, sign-on bonus, and details of the relocation package and benefits. Beyond that, you may be eligible and negotiate for a written severance agreement that typically provides you with six months' to one year's salary in the event of your termination. However, many of today's employment agreements are "at will," which means that employers may terminate your agreement at any time for any reason, provided they are not violating any antidiscrimination laws, and

217

you may resign under the same circumstances. You need to become familiar with your state's laws for termination with cause or without cause.

A change-in-control clause may be an option at the level of middle management and above. This ensures you of compensation in the event your position is eliminated due to a corporate merger, acquisition, or downsizing. The components of the package will vary from company to company and depend upon the level of the executive. Typically, you might be looking at receiving one year's base salary and/or immediate vesting of all granted stock, immediate exercising of all options, payment of all performance bonuses, immediate vesting of your pension benefits, and continuation of your health care benefits and life insurance.

Similarly, noncompete agreements can be quite complicated and vary in restrictions, length of time, and from state to state. Noncompete restrictions are designed to prevent you from using confidential company information to benefit a competitor, soliciting clients from your former firm, or recruiting employees from your prior place of employment.

Top-level executives who might have complex and detailed contracts typically employ the services of attorneys who specialize in employment contracts to maximize what they are offered in these types of packages.

At what point do I back down from negotiating?

You need to know when to refrain from making your demands known, or if you're not sure, take the advice from the recruiter when it's time to stop. You need to understand all of the dynamics of the particular negotiations. You might have skills that are in great demand and may have been the only qualified candidate who made it through the interview process—in which case, you have greater negotiating power. However, if you push too hard, you risk appearing arrogant, greedy, or unreasonable. What happened to the congenial candidate the prospective employer interviewed? If you believe you have achieved all that you can expect to achieve during the negotiations, then it's time to make a decision to stop and wait for a response or walk away from the offer if it doesn't meet your expectations. Even if the hiring executive meets all of your demands because he desperately needs to fill a position, you may have done irreparable harm to your career with your new boss, for he may feel that you used undue pressure to get what you wanted. *Don't* risk starting a new job on the wrong foot! Remember, employment is an ongoing relationship, and how you handle the initial negotiations will impact you as an employee during your tenure with the company. View negotiating as the start of a long-term relationship during which there will be many future opportunities for rewards.

How much notice do I give the company when I leave my current position? Is two weeks enough?

The general rule for giving your employers notice that you are leaving your job is two weeks. However, you do not want to burn bridges with your former employers, particularly if you expect a good reference from them. Your timing should be such that you don't jeopardize your new opportunity while at the same time not leaving your supervisors or subordinates to pick up the pieces in the midst of a major project or crisis. Use your best judgment.

Issues You May Need to Overcome That Can Weaken Your Negotiating Power

A prospective employer might look for ways to weaken your negotiating power. Although she might not raise these issues with you directly, it is someone's job to find bargaining tools to work in the company's favor. If a recruiter or prospective employer hits you with these perceived red flags, you don't want to appear apologetic or agree that because of this or that you should accept a lower compensation. To strengthen your negotiating position, you should proactively arm yourself with the right kind of knowledge and be prepared for a dialogue that addresses the proposed issues.

Age

Many mid- and late-career job seekers may face being perceived as having low energy or being too expensive or unable to learn new technology. When meeting with recruiters or hiring executives, emphasize points that highlight your youthful vigor, such as completion of a 5K run or a seminar in online stock trading. I've met many 30-year-olds who have a much lower energy level than candidates in their 60s. It's an issue of mind-set. If you possess the intangible assets I outlined in Chapter 7, you will appear ageless to the prospective employer. And if you are perceived as being too expensive, demonstrate the value that you bring to the table from your years of experience, not that you have reached your salary level based solely on longevity in a position. You might also mention programs you have completed that have broadened your skills and enhance your value. Candidates who appear too young may need to overcome similar issues. Don't stretch your qualifications but emphasize accomplishments and what results your strategies garnered for the department and the company.

Gender

Dealing with the gender gap can be a difficult challenge in negotiating your compensation package. Many human resource professionals subscribe to salary surveys and won't budge on the numbers they have in print in their trusty files. In the 2000 salary survey conducted by *Working Woman* magazine, the editors state that "the deck is still stacked against women in the wage game." Unfortunately, women's compensation can be skewed downward due to real-life factors that these surveys don't take into account. Therefore, the woman who leaves the workforce to have a child and write a book that could enhance her marketability can be penalized. She did not take one year off to lounge in a hammock and drink mint juleps. She maintained her business contacts and kept current professionally. If this scenario has any ring of truth for you, be prepared to deal with it when negotiating your compensation package. But, again, always be realistic and keep your ego in check.

Career Gap
Similar to being stigmatized by gender, a gap in your resume can be hard to explain. Why? Because you are looking for ways to cover it up. Be honest and forthcoming in explaining the employment gap in your resume. If you were laid off and had a difficult time finding a new opportunity, state why. Perhaps you were looking for work during a recession or needed to take time off to care for a terminally ill parent. Taking time out to write a book, travel, or raise a family isn't a career killer if you've remained fresh in your profession and maintained your contacts. A career killer is if you lie about the gap.

Career Mulligans
As I mentioned in prior chapters, career mulligans are career missteps: positions you've accepted that, for whatever reason, did not prove to be all you anticipated, and you resigned after serving a couple of months. Prospective employers will usually understand career mulligans. However, you need to be prepared to discuss why the situation didn't work out, not just dismiss it with a wave of the hand and an under-your-breath comment. Take a proactive stance in discussing it. Demonstrate what you learned from this perceived failure.

With One Company Too Long/Job-Hopping
If you have been with the same company for, let's say, 10 years or longer, your marketplace value may be diminished while your total compensation in your current position may have exceeded what your prospective employer is willing to offer

you. And you may be perceived as being too rigid, risk averse, comfortable, or complacent. Or you might be seen as wanting to approach your work at the new company just as things were done at your prior company. You need to demonstrate in the interview that you can deal with uncertainty and rapid change and provide concrete examples of how you have done so. Prudent job-hopping is no longer perceived as a stigma in today's hiring market. If your career has taken a more adventurous route—assignments with a number of companies in different industries—you may actually have greater marketplace value and negotiating power. Zigzagging up the ladder gives you perceived broader capabilities. However, if you've changed jobs every few months, you will most likely have a little more explaining to do!

Workaholism versus a Balanced Life

Striking a balance between your professional life and your personal life can make you an attractive candidate as long as you don't tip the scales too far in one direction to position yourself as one or the other. You might fear that if your prospective employer perceives you to be a workaholic, you'll score lower than another, more balanced candidate. To counteract this perception, you may launch into a lengthy discussion of your family and outside interests. This monologue could make the interviewer question when you might fit work into your schedule! Conversely, if you have personal obligations that take you away from the office frequently, your new boss will take a dim view of you omitting this information during the interview process and then springing your needs on her once you are hired. Use your best judgment in portraying your work style, and optimally the corporate culture will allow you the flexibility to strike a balance.

All Things Being Equal . . .

It has become much more complicated to negotiate a job offer in today's corporate America, where long-term employees are earning far less than their newly hired counterparts. The new compensation paradigms of the past decade have distorted the rules of peer equity. However, if you have mapped out your goals, determined your marketplace value, and appreciate the limitations and requirements of the prospective employer, arriving at an agreeable compensation arrangement should be a relatively easy matter. Remember, nothing can take the place of years of experience, maturity, judgment, and wisdom, no matter what the economy or hiring market.

———

Secret: Start high. You can always negotiate down, but you cannot negotiate up. Allow me to paraphrase the words of comedian Steve Martin: How do you make one million dollars and not pay taxes? First, make the million dollars and then worry about paying Uncle Sam.

Referencing– The Strategy Behind Not Selecting Your Best Friend to Vouch for You

Who, What, When, Where, and How?

I'm borrowing these hallmarks of journalism basics from my college years to emphasize just how important it is for you to know the facts about referencing. *Whom* do you choose to be your references, *what* is a reference, *when* do you submit them and to whom, *where* does the information go next, and *how* does the referencing process work? Selecting the right individuals to serve as your references and maintaining good relationships with them is absolutely and without question one of the most critical pieces in the search process puzzle, not only to support your candidacy for one job but also as an essential component of your overall career navigation.

Let me cite two examples of why is it so important for you to have good references. By *good references* I mean people who think and speak highly of your character and you as a professional. These individuals are willing to go out on a limb for you and confirm for the recruiter and hiring authority that you are capable of performing in a leadership capacity all of the responsibilities deemed necessary for the position you are seeking. They are willing to risk their own reputation by affirming that you can and will uphold the high standard to which you are being held by the recruiter's assessment. If the reference tells the recruiter that your performance was stellar and your character flawless and you prove to be the opposite, the individual's reputation will be tarnished by you in what always is a very small community.

During my tenure as a headhunter to date, I've had only one or two candidates worthy of placement who have *not* had good references. One such incident involved a candidate whom I had spoken with over the years. He had all of the characteristics and qualifications that a recruiter would want in a strong candidate. I had spoken with him about a number of opportunities, but due to family commitments he was reluctant to relocate from the major metropolitan area in which he lived and worked. As a senior-level executive in a particular niche function, his options were fairly limited without relocating. However, he was open to looking at potential opportunities because the company for which he worked was small and he was seeking to broaden his capabilities within a larger organization.

When I had an assignment in his city that I felt was a solid opportunity for him, I contacted him, and his response was tremendously enthusiastic. I presented him to my client on the panel of semifinalists and, as I anticipated, the client executives determined that he met all of the qualifications and cultural-fit criteria that were crucial to succeeding at this multibillion-dollar manufacturing company. My candidate interviewed with all of the executive members of the company's search committee, and each was ecstatic about his candidacy. I was as well. My client decided to extend an offer, and we began hammering out all of the details. During this time I began checking the candidate's references. Now I felt pretty confident that this next step would be routine, as I had already conducted preliminary stealth references, and each contact raved about his integrity and performance as a first-rate professional. My stealth contacts were people I had known over the years and whose opinion I held in high regard. As expected, when we completed the reference checking, all came back glowing.

However, there was one more contact the client suggested we call—a professional whom the client knew and who had served as a supervisor of our candidate in a previous position he'd had. I personally spoke with this individual, and he took a dim view of this candidate's professionalism and overall work performance. He said this individual was not a team player and would never work well with Company X's senior management or pretty much anyone in the organization. We asked for specifics as to why he felt this way, and he cited several. I delivered this information to the client who said the individual had given her the bad news directly as well. With this kind of poor reference, the candidate was ruled out almost instantaneously. There was no turning back, even though seven other professionals had given him superior references. The candidate had reached the point of the offer letter only to have the imminent union collapse due to one poor reference. Think for a moment about the reality of how crushing that was to all parties concerned—after months of searching and interviewing, there was nothing but disappointment on all fronts. One bad reference can also prove deadly to your future. The truly unfortunate aspect of this situation is that I personally knew not only the candidate for many years prior to involving him in a search but also his former boss and all the politics tied to their relationship. And, to this day, I am confident the negative reference was rooted in politics, not truth. After all, seven other professionals had given him a resounding endorsement, not to mention the positive stealth (or behind-the-scenes, highly confidential references) I had already conducted prior to presenting him to the client! Now I won't blackball this candidate from all future searches I am conducting, as I feel this reference was circumstantial. However, it definitely supports the notion of being careful about walking a straight line for one's career path and making all decisions with integrity.

Maintaining contact with your references will not only help you at the time of a job offer but may also lead you to other opportunities. Suppose you've decided that you've accomplished all of your intended goals in your current job, you work in a small department or business unit, your immediate supervisor doesn't plan to vacate his position in the near future, and you don't see any options for a next best career step within your present company. It's time for you to seek a more challenging opportunity. Here's what I suggest you do. Contact your former supervisor who has moved to a competitor company and reacquaint yourself with her. Advise this individual that you are launching a job search and ask if she would serve as a reference for you when the time comes. The professional is happy to do so and, by the way, knows of an opportunity in which you might be interested at a Silicon Valley high-tech company. "Give them a call and mention my name." See how it works? These are two good reasons for you to identify and nurture solid relationships with your references, they are why I coach the candidates with whom I work to *always* stay in touch with these individuals who have the power to move your career forward. You want to remain fresh in their minds at all times.

What Is a Reference?

By now you probably know what a reference is. However, let me make it perfectly clear so that we are all on the same page, so to speak. Let's look at *The American Heritage Dictionary of the English Language,* Fourth Edition, definition of *reference* as it relates to a job search: "a.) A person who is in a position to recommend another or vouch for his or her fitness, as for a job; b.) A statement about a person's qualifications, character, and dependability."

Essentially, references are those individuals a recruiter or hiring authority contacts for testimony as to a candidate's character, background, and overall qualifications for a specific opportunity to obtain an independent and objective evaluation of the candidate. The recruiter will have assessed a candidate and determined that he may be qualified for a certain assignment and then affirms her assessment of the candidate's abilities with the references' comments.

Whom Do You Choose to Be a Reference?

Choosing a reference is very simple for some candidates who know the drill and have a ready list prepared to give the recruiter. If you are a candidate who has not experienced the referencing process, you might think that it's appropriate to submit the people who know you best. These contacts would likely be your best friend; your spouse; your parents; an uncle; a cousin; your sister; a military buddy; a pastor, priest, or rabbi; your trusted confidant, or someone else you have known for many years. Although these individuals may be sources of positive information on your personal life, they are *not* appropriate references to vouch for your professional experience, as it is highly unlikely that any of them have worked alongside you in a corporate environment. And even if they have also worked with you, they may not prove to be as credible a reference as others you might provide the recruiter.

In short, if you are being considered for a job, your list should include five or six individuals with whom you have interfaced in your professional life, most of whom should be related to your current or previous employment. Over the years, you have developed and nurtured myriad business-related contacts who have seen you in action at work and could serve as a reference for you. Within companies for which you have worked, these individuals ideally would be a former direct supervisor, another senior-level manager with whom you interfaced on projects, a trusted peer who knows of your accomplishments, and a subordinate whom you feel has the maturity to judge your capabilities. References outside the company may be vendors with whom you worked on many projects or, more important, mentors and confidants who have nurtured you over the years, witnessed your career ascent, and may be able to assess your abilities from a growth and momentum perspective.

If you have worked at one company for many years, it may seem a daunting task to provide references from your current place of employment without disclosing that you are seeking another position, which ultimately may jeopardize your job. Clearly, this is not wise. Every headhunter would prefer to speak with your current supervisor, but most often that is just not possible. In this instance you would want to identify former supervisors who have been promoted or assigned to another division or left the company, others within the company in another department who have become close confidants and know your work, and other mentors. This is a situation where having a mentor becomes so important. (I'll discuss the concept of having a mentor in the next chapter.) If you refuse to allow the recruiter to contact anyone in your current company, it will raise doubts about your interpersonal skills and overall employment. Certainly there's *someone* whom you trust and in whom you have confided within your present company—someone who respects you and may want the best for your future, or an individual who will not be impacted by your departure may also be a logical choice.

Suppose you have just left a company and are in between jobs. It is in your best interest to identify a former immediate supervisor who will attest to your good employment; not doing so may raise a red flag to the recruiter and hiring executives that you left on other than ideal terms. If there are legal issues surrounding the terms of your departure and your former boss can't speak to anyone about your employment, it's incumbent upon you to find someone in the organization who will speak to your high standing in the company.

In addition to the four or five "core" references you choose to submit to the recruiter, there are several reasons why you should identify a few more who will serve your referencing needs. Suppose the recruiter is working under tight time constraints to submit your references to the client hiring executives. Three out of five of your references are unavailable. One is on a safari in Africa, another is in the midst of the annual shareholder's meeting, and the third is undergoing surgery. Or maybe one or two just can't be reached because a cell phone isn't connecting. Two references are not enough to give an accurate portrayal of your qualifications. Do you scramble to line up three more professionals with whom you haven't spoken in years? No. Because you anticipated this might happen, you have several others on your list who will be happy to vouch for your good character and professional performance. Another good reason to have more than a handful of references is to demonstrate your confidence that any one of several high-profile individuals will be more than happy to share their wealth of knowledge about your outstanding performance in any number of situations and settings! A third reason to compile a broad range of references is that you may be pursuing a position that requires a unique set of qualifications that are slightly outside your area of expertise. The recruiter will want professionals who can speak to your experience in a certain function or industry as well as your ability to move into another area.

Let me give you my perspective on both the type of professionals and the components of each reference that headhunters are looking for when you submit them to us. This guideline will help you in shaping your list of qualified references.

1. *Name:* You might have known someone as Jack or Annie. Give the contact's full, legal name or the name he or she uses professionally. And use the proper form of address—Mr., Ms., or Dr.—so there is no doubt as

to the individual's gender if it's Pat, Chris, or Leslie, and we want to give proper respect to someone who has earned his or her Ph.D. or M.D. Ideally, you should indicate "Mr. John D. Smith" or "Dr. Anne H. Jones," with a notation in parentheses as to his or her common name, if relevant.

2. *Title:* List the reference's current title as well as the position he or she held when you worked together. Spell titles out in full so there will be no confusion as to meaning, particularly in light of some of today's new and creative titles. Also, if the person's title is senior vice president or vice president and so on, provide the name of the department he or she oversaw (i.e., was it marketing, operations, manufacturing, or technology, and so on).

The composition of contacts we're seeking as references includes the following:

- *Your immediate supervisors:* Ideally, we'd prefer to talk with one or two and possibly more immediate supervisors from your prior positions. We understand if you are unable to provide your current immediate supervisor, so it becomes critical for us to contact former supervisors to verify that you were in good standing in your prior positions. You may also wish to provide your former immediate supervisor's boss, if he had direct contact with you and can speak to your experience. Include two or three references from this category. And by the way, you could also arrange for the recruiter or hiring executive to contact your current supervisor once you are designated as the top candidate for a particular position. This will then protect your confidentiality significantly but will also ultimately provide the prospective employer with information she prefers to have.
- *Heads of other departments/business units:* It helps to paint a well-rounded picture of you if you are

able to show some cross-functional experience in your background and have executives from other areas of the company vouch for it. Perhaps you interfaced with members of senior management when your company went public, launched a new operating group, or navigated a merger or acquisition. You may have had extensive exposure to the company's chief legal officer or head of operations. Don't hesitate to include this stratum of management on your list. Include at least two references from this category.

- *Members of boards of directors:* Particularly if you are a CEO or other corporate officer, you will want to include members of your board of directors as key individuals for headhunters to contact. Include those whom you believe will provide the best perspective on your candidacy in your industry or as it best relates to the prospective employer's needs. Include one or two references from this category if it applies to you.
- *Corporate peers:* You might find that your peers in an organization can provide the best perspective on your accomplishments as they may have worked side by side with you and saw firsthand the depth of your contribution to the overall goals of the company or a specific endeavor. Even if your peers have a different area of focus than you, they will have seen your piece of the puzzle that created the final work. Include at least two references from this category.
- *Subordinates:* Well-selected subordinates are another group of individuals who can attest to your capabilities firsthand. Although they may not be at the level to fully understand your technical abilities, they will be able to respond to questions about such issues as your management style and leadership qualities, essentially speaking to what kind of boss you were to them. When you identify subordinates, be sure they fully understand what it means to be a reference,

that they are mature, and will keep in confidence your job search, even if they are former subordinates—which they most likely will be! Include at least two references from this category.

- *Customers, suppliers, vendors, and other third-party business contacts:* A satisfied customer or vendor can be among your best references, as they can provide testimony of your professional behavior and the respect you command outside the company. The recruiter will see through anyone who gives you a good reference to entice a favor from you. So in making your selection, identify business contacts who have nothing to gain from showering you with praise and who know your abilities. Include one or two references from this category.

- *Mentors:* Choose the individuals who have watched you grow in your career and who know your current level of seniority. Mentors can provide the recruiter with a depth of knowledge about your background that other references may not be able to. Your mentors may also fall into one of the other previously listed categories. Include two references from this category.

You may have personal relationships with some of these references. That's okay. They know you professionally as well. However, you want to stay away from giving references that you know only through social contact, and stay away from giving contacts that are relatives. Former professors are fine, but list them only if you've remained in contact with them since your college days and they can speak adeptly about your recent accomplishments.

3. *Company:* Give the full name of the reference's current company and a line as to what size and type of business it is. If the reference now works for a different company than when you worked together, list the

name of the company for which you both worked. Give the city and state of the company.

4. *Your relationship:* Describe the nature of your professional relationship with each reference when you worked together. Even though the person's title may appear to provide that information, it's not always clear without some descriptor. Was the contact your immediate supervisor, your subordinate, or a senior executive within your business unit, or did you report directly to this individual? If it is a third-party business contact, identify how the two of you interact, that is, if you hired the public relations agency and managed the relationship or if you brought in the customer or client. It will help put the reference in context for us.

5. *Length of time acquainted:* It's also important to identify the number of years you and the reference have known one another *and* worked together. You might have known someone for 15 years but only worked together for 1 of those years. This information helps put your references into perspective for the recruiter and client executives, particularly if one reference's comments have a more personal slant, or it will explain why the individual might not know something about your background.

6. *Contact information:* Essential to the recruiter checking your references is their being reachable in a timely manner. It's better to provide us with more contact information than you believe we'll need than not enough. Please list telephone numbers—work, home, and cell phone, if you have them; pager number, if available; and e-mail address and street address. It would be helpful for you to indicate how best to get in touch with your references and perhaps include a secretary's name and number or those of some other individual who may be of help in scheduling a time to talk to the individual.

When compiling your list of references, keep in mind that a recruiter wants to see both recent contacts and some from positions you held a few years ago. However, if you reach back too far in your career or only provide contacts from the past couple of years, it might raise suspicion as to what from those periods of time you may feel you don't want known to an executive recruiter or prospective employer.

When Do You Submit References and to Whom?

The recruiter will advise you when it's time to submit your list of references. By the time you are asked for your list, you will have most likely been through one or two rounds of interviews with the client executives. The recruiter will call and tell you that you've been identified as the finalist candidate, or possibly one of two finalists, and the next step is to conduct formal reference checking. Keep in mind that the recruiter may have already conducted informal reference checks, or stealth references, on your background prior to this point in the process. If these references were not positive, you would not have been moved forward in the search.

At this point you will provide the recruiter with your full list of references or an edited list of those contacts whom you believe can best portray your abilities and accomplishments as they relate to the position you are seeking. If the recruiter begins contacting them and they are not available, be prepared to shift to your secondary reference contacts and have them ready if the recruiter requests them.

Should you list your references on your resume? It's not necessary to do so. Recruiters and hiring authorities do not expect to see references until closer to the point in time when you become either one of the top two candidates or *the* top candidate. In fact, if you are in the midst of a job search and you include your list of references with every resume that you send out, you run the risk of people contacting your references too often, and you could burn them out. Besides, if you accompany your reference list with your resume, what point are you trying to make? Is it because you believe your resume won't stand on its own merit and you need to prop it up with impressive names? Many recruiters and company executives know management in other companies. They may ask you about these individuals or contact them themselves to see what they will say about you anyway. Remember, if your contacts are called repeatedly, they may feel imposed upon and tire of serving as a reference for you. Use them sparingly.

How the Recruiter Conducts a Reference Check and *Where* the Information Goes

Typically a retained recruiter will conduct a thorough reference check on the candidate, using a combination of references he submitted, as well as stealth references. The recruiter is usually the one who conducts the reference-checking portion of the process, but sometimes the in-house corporate recruiter or human resource representative at the client company may choose to perform this step.

The process is quite simple. Once the recruiter has your list of references, she will review it and select four or five who will most likely provide a candid, responsible, and accurate testimonial of your character and professional abilities. Most often this is conducted by telephone. The recruiter will have a list of 10 to 20 questions that will include some basic relationship-based information, such as how the reference has known the candidate, for how long they have been acquainted, how long he was with the company, and how the two interacted. The remainder queries will be directly related to the position the candidate is pursuing. An example of some questions include:

- How would you describe Steve's management style?
- How would you describe his greatest strengths?
- What areas of improvement or development do you see for Steve?

- How would you describe his greatest accomplishment?
- How would you rate Steve's communication skills (both verbal and written presentations)?
- How does Steve manage stress?
- What kind of leader is Steve; how does he motivate people?
- Did Steve meet his department's and company's goals during his tenure?
- How would you describe his ability to make judgment calls, and can you provide examples?
- How did other senior members of management/peers/subordinates/outside business contacts view him as a professional?
- What type of counselor was he to senior management?
- Tell me about his global experience.
- Does he have a strong grasp of his industry/function/technology?
- What advice would you give him to help with future career growth?
- What was the pace and culture like at your company when the two of you worked together?
- Is there anything you believe prevented Steve from doing his job and meeting or exceeding management's expectations?
- Under what terms did Steve leave the company?
- Would you hire him again?
- Is there anything else I should know about Steve?

The recruiter will take notes during the telephone conversation and from these notes prepare a summary of each reference given. It is most firms' practice not to attribute the quotes to any one individual for legal reasons. At my firm, we write a four- to six-page reference commentary document that summarizes our findings. We prepare this document for the client and review it with the hiring executives, emphasizing points we may feel are of particular importance, and we will address areas the client or we felt necessary to probe in the reference process. At this time, the client will either be satisfied with the reference checking or will ask us to explore in greater detail specific areas of concern; however, this is usually the exception rather than the rule.

The following pages portray an abbreviated representative sample of a hypothetical candidate's reference commentary.

Mr. Stephen (Steve) S. Stevens Reference Commentary

"I have the highest regard for Steve. He is one of the few professionals at his level that I think very highly of. Just before his promotion to the ABC Group, I tried to hire him. I would hire him in any top spot in a large corporation or to head a major business unit."

"Without question, I see Steve being a stellar performer in a top global role. He's a very strong leader."

"He's a very effective counselor to senior management. He keeps a cool head under pressure, thinks strategically, and does what he thinks is best. He will give you his point of view and push back with conviction. I've seen him disagree and win, and disagree and lose. And he's won more than he's lost. However, if the CEO makes a decision in the end, he will support it wholeheartedly."

"He would do a great job for any leading corporation. He has the maturity, judgment, and experience for this type of position. He has strong leadership skills and global expertise. He also has great experience working for one of the leading technology companies in the world. I can't think of a more well-rounded candidate for the job."

"Steve's a very bright individual. He absolutely has the intellectual capital he needs to manage a global position for any complex company. He's also driven."

"Steve is a pro. He's tough but also very professional in his demeanor. He'll go to the mat for what he believes in. But he's diplomatic about it, too. He's appropriately aggressive for a top job."

(continued)

(continued)

"Steve is very comfortable to be with. He's great at building relationships with any group he interacts with. He's highly skilled at getting to the meat of the matter and addressing it with just the right approach—with numerous constituencies."

"He fully understands how to work within a matrix management structure. He's a great leader."

"He's very forthright. There's no hidden agenda with Steve."

"I would say his subordinates have the highest regard for him. I've seen him interact with his team and you could see the mutual respect between them."

"I truly cannot think of an area of improvement for Steve. There's nothing I saw lacking in him as a professional, or on a personal level. He's a rock-solid individual."

"Steve would do a great job at X Corporation and fit in with its culture. He's driven, he's bright, he's polished; he's an overall top-notch professional. His technology background is a big plus."

"There's nothing negative I can say about Steve except maybe he should take more time off. He thrives on a challenge."

"His ability to counsel was excellent when he reported to me. He's firm and has a depth of good judgment you don't always see. He's confident in his guidance."

"Steve came into a difficult situation at [the company]. We had just made a significant acquisition, and the employees from the company we acquired were very angry. Steve personally visited employees of the acquired company, quelled their concerns, and mobilized the organization to rally around during this critical time. His proactive efforts were of tremendous value to our organization. He's a strong leader and has great instincts about how to approach a crisis, or any situation for that matter."

"Steve functions very well under stress. He's flexible and adaptable. When he went overseas for [our company], he thrived in a foreign environment. And when he returned, he didn't skip a beat."

(continued)

(continued)

"There is no counsel I would give Steve. He's content when he's in the top spot, and he needs to be challenged. A number-one position is what keeps him happy."

"I give him my highest recommendation for a number-one position at any Fortune 10 company."

"Steve is one of the most outstanding professionals who ever reported to me. He's been doing extremely well ever since that time."

"Steve was one of the 'anointed ones' at ABC Company. He was just a kid when he joined [the company], but at that young age you could see that he had the maturity, the right temperament, skills, and tenacity to succeed. After just one year with [the company], he was hand-picked to launch a major business unit."

"Steve is a true leader. He's an engaging person, and a great consensus builder. When he joined [the company], there was a real culture clash between employees who were accustomed to the old way of doing things and those who brought in a new perspective. Steve was among the latter. He didn't bowl them over and force his ideas upon them, but instead rallied them around him with intelligence and logic and won them over to his side."

"My boss at [the company] literally said to me about Steve, 'We're watching the making of a real star.' He really blossomed at [the company] and in his subsequent positions at other companies. He's one of the few professionals I'd contact again to work for me."

"He has a thick skin. He's flexible and knows how to counsel senior management."

"Steve really understands the technology industry."

"He ensures a company's image isn't tarnished along the route to higher profits."

"If restructuring is involved, it can be a painful process, but I've seen Steve manage that process firmly and with sensitivity. He is open and frank, yet diplomatic. He has great people skills."

(continued)

(continued)

"One of his strong suits is crisis management. At [the company] we were constantly dealing with crises."

"Steve is tenacious. When he oversaw the Asia Pacific region at our company, he worked 24/7. He was the first person to head up this newly created region and he pulled it together beautifully and thrived in the role."

"Steve is extremely dynamic. He's an equally strong presenter one-on-one and before hundreds of people. He's a very high energy individual. Very polished."

"Changing industries is no problem for Steve. He moved effortlessly from manufacturing to technology. He's very bright."

"Steve knows how to build solid business relationships."

REFERENCES CONTACTED

MR. GEORGE G. GEORGE, CHAIRMAN, XYZ COMPANY (NEW YORK, NY): George has known Steve for several years. When Mr. George was vice chairman and COO at XYZ Company, Steve had just joined the company as a senior manager in Asian-Pacific operations. He later reported to him for four years.

MR. CHARLIE C. CHARLES, CHIEF OPERATIONS OFFICER, THE ZZZ COMPANY (CHICAGO, IL): Charlie has known Steve 20-plus years. Steve reported to Charlie during a portion of his more than 10 years with [the company], and they have connected regularly over the years.

MS. ROBERTA R. ROBERTS, SENIOR VICE PRESIDENT, MARKETING, THE RRR COMPANY (NEW YORK, NY): Steve and Roberta have known one another for 12 years. They are peers at RRR Company and currently serve together as corporate officers.

MR. JOHN (JACK) J. JOHNS, PRESIDENT, GLOBAL COMPANY (MINNEAPOLIS, MN): John was a customer of Steve's when he was head of sales at ZZZ Company. They have known each other for 15 years.

(continued)

> *(continued)*
> MS. SUZANNE S. SUSAN, MANAGER, TELEMARKETING,
> RRR COMPANY (NEW YORK, NY): Suzanne is one of
> Steve's direct reports and oversees the telemarketing
> department, one of several departments Steve oversees in
> operations.

As you can see, the reference-checking process is very straightforward. In this sample for a hypothetical senior-level operations-oriented position, the candidate is portrayed as a strong leader and solid counselor to senior management with solid management and decision-making skills, among many other attributes. And his former immediate supervisors would hire him again. None of the references said he had any areas that need improvement, which is something that we always probe. This example is a very positive and balanced reference.

What Does the Recruiter and Hiring Executive Want to Hear?

The search professional wants evidence from credible and respected sources that the candidate has performed as well in current or prior positions in support of his or her assessment. The hiring authority wants the same level of comfort, and past history is one of the few methods of gauging future performance. If all of our questions are readily answered by the references without hesitation and are positive and balanced, it adds to our arsenal of statistics about the validity and credibility of the candidate we have proposed to our clients.

Should You Notify or Coach Your References?

How do you help your references to be a successful part of the process? Ideally, you would have remained in touch with your references over the years, so you should not need to expend much energy setting them up for a recruiter's call. In general, you should get in touch with them the moment you launch your job search. As I mentioned earlier in this chapter, they may be able to refer you to an opportunity. If you call them at the point of the offer, you should definitely notify them about the job you are vying for and at what company, the name of the recruiter— and a bit about his background and that of the search firm— and when they might expect a call from the search professional. You don't want them to be caught off guard.

It's not a good idea to "color" your references' opinions about you ... don't write their script. Why? Because if recruiters are good at what they do, they will uncover the set up, and it will reflect negatively on you. Be sure that when you contact your references to send them a copy of your current resume and review it with them. Take a few minutes to refresh their memory of some of your high points, particularly if the reference was not an immediate supervisor, direct report, or other professional with whom you did not have daily contact. You'll want to make your references' job as easy as possible, and be certain they have enough information about you so that when the recruiter calls, they will not give one- or two-word responses. You'll want your references to be as honest and as expansive as possible about your background and experience.

What about Reference Letters?

Letters of recommendation or reference letters can be an excellent tool in support of your candidacy, but they cannot take the place of the reference-checking process that a recruiter or hiring executive conducts. Letters of reference can be outdated and might not address the best qualities or key experiences of the candidate, information that the prospective employer is

244

seeking. If you were fired from a job, letters of reference may be helpful, as many companies will not give a reference and not even discuss a termination, as their policy will allow them only to provide employment basics, such as dates of employment, title, responsibilities and to whom the individual reported. As part of a severance agreement, a former employer might provide the terminated employee with a scripted reference statement that confirms the basics in writing. Regardless of what letters you may have to support your claims of employment, you must be honest in discussing why and under what circumstances you left each position. Don't forget, as I mentioned earlier in this book, that honesty is always the best policy.

What's the Proper Follow-Up Protocol with References?

Ask the recruiter what contacts she reached as part of the reference checking and then call or write them and thank them for their time. They have performed a valuable service to you, and you want to remain in good standing with them. It's all part of relationship building and professionalism in navigating your career.

Background, Drug and Physical Checks, and Psychological Tests—Part of Referencing?

A recruiter is generally responsible and equipped for reference checking. If the client determines that a deeper assessment is required of a candidate, either because there is some doubt regarding the qualifications of the candidate or as part of the company's standard procedure in assessing executives, the service will be performed by outside consultants.

The Legal Side of Reference Checking

There are two primary goals in checking references: To verify factual matters, such as start date, when the employee left the company, job title, to whom he reported, and salary; and to verify qualitative characteristics, such as performance on the job, strengths, weaknesses, leadership abilities, interpersonal skills, and so on. When recruiting for an executive-level position, verifying information beyond "just the facts" is critical to a prospective employer to lessen the risk in hiring at that level. Unless the candidate has provided the recruiter with his own list of references, the recruiter would be limited to speaking with a human resource representative of the company to check references. And on the advice of legal counsel, companies typically have a "no comment policy," allowing only verification of basic information, such as start and end date, and job title, as I mentioned previously. Some companies will not even release salary information, even with a signed release from the former employee. Employers who give any information beyond the basics can face lawsuits alleging defamation. Even if a positive reference is given, the former employer risks legal action from the new employer if negative information about the employee is left out and he performs poorly in the new role. The general rule today is that when an employer does provide a reference, the good and bad must be fully disclosed. Otherwise, no reference should be provided at all. To lessen their risk, some firms employ a 900-number telephone service through which employment verifications are conducted by a computerized voice or contact firms that conduct reference-checking services.

There are state and federal laws regulating what can and can't be asked about a former employee, and recruiters and hiring executives know their limitations in the questions they can ask when conducting reference checking. However, be smart about the fact that if a recruiter excels at what they do, they will know how to discern the information they need from myriad marketplace sources—not just your reference list!

The End Goal

The end goal for all parties involved in a reference-checking exercise is to have both client and candidate feel satisfied that the agreement into which they will be entering is the next best career step for the candidate and that the prospective employer is hiring the best candidate for the job. Your role in reaching this end goal is to provide the recruiter with as much information about you and your qualifications during the interview and reference-checking process, and by so doing, you'll reach your goal.

———

Secret: Okay, so maybe this is no secret, but as the saying goes: "It's not what you know, it's who you know." As you navigate your career, the personal networks you develop will greatly influence your ultimate destination.

CHAPTER 12

The Mentor Factor
The Secrets to Developing Effective Relationships with Mentors

Developing and nurturing mentoring relationships throughout your professional life is one of the most important practices to master in successfully navigating your career. I have mentioned the notion of mentoring numerous times throughout this book, as I believe it is critical to secure and leverage a relationship with a mentor, and it's too often overlooked as a strategy in seeking a new opportunity or in defining and expanding one's career.

Why is it that the concept of mentoring eludes some, whereas other, more enlightened individuals have embraced the practice—and as a result have gained significant professional fulfillment as either a mentor or a mentee or both? I believe that part of the lack of awareness about this practice stems from the fact that so many in the workplace today move like robots from their computer monitor at the office to their television screen at home and have lost critical interpersonal skills that foster a desire for such relationships. Conversely, these are skills others have mastered and rely upon in developing both personal and professional relationships. Others may simply not want to hear "the good, bad, and indifferent" as it relates to their professional strengths and weaknesses.

If this human component is missing from your strategy, my best advice to you as you launch your job search or strive to evolve in your career is to change your behavior. Make time to get away from your electronic gadgetry, the Internet, the VCR, your CD player, your television set, and even the movie theater and ensure that mentoring becomes a critical part of your professional development. Although it's important to employ these electronic tools as a means of learning and communication, don't limit yourself to them in your career journey. Face-to-face, human-being-to-human-being learning can be far more rewarding and fulfilling than what you gain from staring at a monitor in search of guidance. Candidates I know who have participated in a corporate mentoring program or have taken the initiative to seek mentor relationships on their own have been able to gain a solid foothold in their chosen functional discipline and/or industry early in their career and to sustain their lead as they have grown professionally. People who have mentors want to succeed. They are generally proactive and enterprising and are in search of seeking networking opportunities early in their career, and recruiters immediately know how this has positively impacted these professional careers.

Today's Mentor Programs Are Broader Than Those of Yesteryear

The concept of mentoring has evolved over the years to become much broader and more sophisticated than in prior decades.

Indeed, the term *mentor* reaches far back in history, originating from ancient Greece. Odysseus, a king of Ithaca and the Greek leader in the Trojan War, entrusted his friend Mentor with educating his son. In more recent civilization, mentoring has become synonymous with coaching, tutoring, and guiding and has continually evolved with our everchanging world. Over the decades mentoring has expanded into the teaching curricula in academia and into corporate training programs in the business arena. However, the days of grooming the protégés to become executive clones are long gone. Today's dynamic mentoring programs embrace change, are cross-generational and cross-cultural, draw laterally and vertically in an organization, and empower the employee to reach beyond the obvious to achieve career success. They address both professional knowledge growth and interpersonal skills development that executives can leverage in the ladder-climbing exercise. These programs enable the individual to work smarter, not harder, and to thrive in any corporate culture and in any economy.

If you work for a corporation that offers mentoring programs, participate in them wholeheartedly. Some companies will assign you a mentor as part of your orientation when you first join. Other companies will link you with "buddies" who can help you with basic operational and procedural knowledge but are not able to serve in the capacity or at the level of mentoring to broaden your experience or guide you in your career. Still others offer mentoring programs that are repackaged training programs and won't encompass the broader counsel that a true mentor can provide you. Or you may be employed at a company that uses outside consulting services to create and execute management, training, and mentoring programs. These consultants address numerous opportunities or issues within an organization, such as employee retention programs, resources for high potential employees or development plans for lackluster employees, cultural and vision development, and general mentoring programs. Explore the programs offered at your company, and if they appear to be worthwhile, volunteer either to be a mentor or to be mentored. Take advantage of these programs and you will find the experience to be tremendously rewarding.

Identifying Mentors Starts with a Self-Inventory

Candidate, know thyself. This phrase should become a mantra in your job search and professional development. I've mentioned throughout this book the importance of the concept as it relates to your career overall, and it has even greater meaning in the process of selecting your mentors. Why? You want to choose individuals whose background is best suited to your growth needs and to guiding you in those areas of development. Identify mentors who have technical abilities where you have weakness, expertise in areas in which you are inexperienced, superior judgment where you are unsure, diverse cultural background where you have a more conventional orientation, or different industry or functional experience to your more narrow focus. The goal of your mentoring program should be to maximize the depth and breadth of your experience. Perhaps your people skills are great, but you've never managed people. You'll want to identify executives who are effective staff managers—optimally, someone who has grown an organization and may have been at the point where you are now in your career when he or she was handed a small department to expand.

You may feel you may only be lacking in one or two areas. In this case, look at the broader scope of mentoring. If you have set down a career path for yourself, identify managers in your organization who have been successful in following this path. Schedule time to have a series of meetings or lunches with them to discuss how they reached their post and what hurdles they might have encountered and overcome along the way. They have been down the path; they know the drill.

In beginning the process of your professional development self-inventory, start with a hard look at your resume and other biographical data to make it simpler to identify your achievements. Talk to your colleagues, friends, and other individuals whom you trust for their perspective on your strengths, weaknesses, and qualities. Then make a chart and list the following as it relates to your background, experience, and behavioral qualities:

- Identify your functional strengths and weaknesses—areas in which you believe you have the most experience and where you lack depth.
- Identify and rank your core competencies, the intangible attributes from Chapter 7.
- Identify your goals and objectives, both long term and short term.

When developing your chart, don't try to be all things to all people. Identify and focus on your tenable strengths and realistic areas of development and your goals that have immediate priority or those on which you can work long term. From this information create your career development plan. Once you have this tangible document at hand, you will be equipped to identify mentors with experience in the areas you have targeted for professional development. These are the mentors who will be best suited to guide you in those areas.

In creating your target list, remember that you are not looking to become a clone of one executive or expect one mentor to satisfy your every requirement. You want to take the best of the best from multiple mentors and begin to formulate your own personal career brand, as I outlined for you in Chapter 8. You'll want to also keep an electronic copy of this chart and update it periodically, along with your assessment of your marketplace value that I discussed in Chapter 10.

In Search of Mentors: Identifying Your Targets

Unless you work for a corporation that offers a mentoring program, how do you develop and nurture your own personal advisory council? If you are familiar with the practice, you are fortunate to have identified certain individuals over the course of your career with whom you have developed a rapport and have grown to trust. You feel you can confide in them on just about any topic. You share with them your aspirations, successes, and shortcomings—both personal and professional. You can rely on them to be a sounding board and to offer advice and counsel both during crises and in day-to-day life. They are your mentors.

For those of you who have not developed a cadre of counselors, where do you begin? Similar to the approach we took in identifying your references in the prior chapter, let's take a look at some of the sources of mentors in your immediate environment.

Inside Your Company

You'll want to approach individuals who have influence in your company. Do they have authority to hire and fire? Do they manage a budget? How large is their staff? Do you see them as sounding board for career and professional issues and as an aid to providing direction in myriad situations? Ask yourself these questions as you review this list.

- *Immediate supervisors:* Some of your immediate mentor targets may be prior supervisors whom you respect and to whom you have always looked for guidance.
- *Your supervisor's supervisor:* You may also identify your boss's boss as someone to approach for more big-picture, global mentoring.
- *Department or line of business heads:* If you seek exposure in specific industries or areas of expertise, target management in those areas, such as manufacturing, operations, strategic development, finance, international, marketing, human resources, and so on.
- *Peers:* It's always important to identify colleagues from other departments or within your group whom you

respect and trust and with whom you have or want to develop a rapport. These individuals may be working on different segments of the same project as you and can offer a different vantage point from yours.

■ *Subordinates:* You may not immediately think of mentors being at any strata below your level of management or having fewer years of experience. However, you might identify an area of weakness in technology or some other area where someone 10 years your junior has strength. Don't feel peculiar about learning from the younger … just because they have fewer years of experience doesn't mean they are inexperienced in all areas. They might have a particular area of expertise in which you are lacking.

Be cognizant of spreading your mentors among different political constituencies in the company. Although this might seem political in and of itself, in the realm of mergers, acquisitions, and terminated CEOs, if you align yourself only with one or two executives or constituencies, when management changes and they're out, you will be, too. This method will also allow you to gather multiple perspectives that will be of broader benefit to you.

Outside Your Company

Take the time and effort to identify professionals from other firms who can provide yet another mentoring perspective for you.

■ *Professional and industry trade organizations:* If you are not a member of a professional or industry trade organization, you should identify the associations that most closely relate to your career path and become a member of one or two immediately. The organizations or associations that will best serve your career needs will be those that relate to your functional expertise or industry of choice. What better choice than to seek advice from these veterans in the discipline and industry you are targeting? Remember, oftentimes these professional organizations have nicely developed mentoring programs.

- *Business clubs:* Many thought leaders and civic-minded individuals are members of these groups and can provide you with a wealth of career advice and counsel. And the club is an ideal location for you to meet.

- *Academia:* Seek former professors who guided you as an undergraduate or in business school. You may also explore what your particular college alumni group offers in mentoring programs, although many of these might be best suited for recent graduates.

- *Community and social organizations:* Although this may not be the optimal source of *professional* mentors, tap into groups in which you are currently involved or plan to become involved. Don't overlook members of athletic clubs, youth groups, fraternal and religious organizations, and charitable organizations. You might want to identify one or two individuals from this group to serve as mentors.

- *Customers, clients, and vendors:* Similar to the approach you take in identifying individuals from this group, use caution in choosing mentors from those who do business with your company. They may be seeking to gain more than you'd like them to gain from the experience.

- *Executive search professionals:* Headhunters can prove to be great mentors when you are a candidate. You may also develop mentoring relationships with them beyond the headhunter-candidate role, as they can give you sound advice on your career and how to approach other mentors!

Every time you attend a networking meeting, seminar, conference, or other event at one of these groups, clubs, or organizations, approach each member with fresh eyes. Get to know a broader segment of the membership and make a target list for your mentoring program. Once you have established a rapport with your target mentors, ask them if they would consider serving in such a role.

Qualities and Characteristics of a Mentor

To help you identify your mentors, you'll want to identify the qualities, type, and level of experience you are seeking in this individual. You'll definitely want them to embody the same qualities of trust and respect and the core competencies that you believe are critical to best serve your career navigation process. What qualities or experience are most important to you?

I've created the following list of 40 attributes and values that you will want your mentors to possess. Many of these qualities are on my list of core competencies in Chapter 7. Now, here's another exercise for you. Take out your pen and rank them in order of priority. With this list and your chart of strengths and areas of development, you'll have the resources you need to make your mentoring selection process more effective.

Trust.
Integrity.
Respect—command, not demand it.
Motivates people to action.
Persuasive.
Inspires others to develop.
Positive attitude.
Good counselor.
Recognizes and rewards success.
Gives clear direction and training in a nurturing, not dictatorial way.
Knows when to leave you to create something yourself.
Understands the value of "we" versus "I."
Natural team builder.
Leads by example.
Doesn't badmouth management, peers, or subordinates.

Makes good hiring decisions.

Good judgment.

Good problem-solving and decision-making abilities.

Provides honest and timely feedback.

Sets realistic goals and objectives.

Is an effective communicator, able to effectively express ideas.

Proactive.

Approachable, open-door policy, makes him- or herself available.

Good listener.

Embraces the new rather than only the tried and true.

Cool under fire.

Sense of humor.

Appropriate level of sensitivity.

Understand business goals and how to meet them.

Leader in functional discipline or industry—solid technical or professional knowledge.

Business mastery.

Vision.

Thinks globally.

Embraces diversity and other cultures.

Intrapreneurial.

Branded career.

Self-confident but not egotistical.

Balance in life.

Passionate.

Enterprising.

How to Approach Mentors and Define the Parameters of the Relationship

Once you've identified your target mentor list, you may find that most executives will embrace the notion and be delighted at the opportunity. Others might bristle at the thought. They may not feel they can carve time out of their schedule at work or that you might take time away from their family. Although the latter is unfortunate for you and for them, as mentoring someone can be a very rewarding experience, you must respect their decision and not feel rejected. Mentoring isn't for everyone. And even the executives who welcome the opportunity to be your mentor might not be able to serve you in that capacity—or at least not in the immediate future. You can't expect your mentoring relationships to happen overnight. They take time to nurture.

There are various ways to approach your prospective mentors with your request. If you know them already, ask them to join you for lunch or some other informal meeting. Explain that you recognize their career achievements and leadership abilities and would like an opportunity to learn from them firsthand. If they are amenable to the idea, schedule a follow-up meeting with them immediately to set the parameters of the relationship and establish a working agreement. Will you meet once or twice a week? once or twice a month? for lunch? after hours? Are casual drop-in visits permitted? What will the length of the mentoring agreement be? a few months? for a particular crisis, issue, or project? How do you both agree when the mentoring is completed?

Be sure to shape your agenda so that there will be no surprises from either party. Identify what you want from the relationship and make it clear to your mentor. Establish realistic and attainable expectations or you will be disappointed in the arrangement.

How to Leverage Your Mentoring Relationships

You may have the MBA, a role with a blue-chip company, and a few years of experience under your belt, but nothing can take the place of the wisdom and maturity that comes from years of experience. The ability to make sound judgment calls grows over time. You may have made some blunders in your job or career and might have had struggled to recover from those mistakes. And you wonder how it could have happened! This is where your mentors enter the picture. They may have made similar mistakes and can provide you with guidance based on their vast business experience. Your mentors will be candid about your strengths and weaknesses and will give you the honest counsel that others might be uncomfortable giving you or might lack interest in doing so. They will provide you with that sounding board that your folks or spouse don't seem to be able to muster. You are looking for objectivity, and objectivity is difficult to draw out of those closest to you. Even your immediate supervisor can't always take an unbiased look at your merits or shortcomings. I believe that if as a rising professional you can master the concept of being mentored, you will find the goals and objectives that you set can be yours to achieve. The powerful effect of mentoring can lead to remarkable results in your career.

What are some of the other ways in which you can leverage your relationship with a mentor? On the practical side, the following are a few of the capacities in which they may serve your needs:

- Create role-playing situations.
- Help you practice your job interviews and debrief following the meetings.
- Encourage you to embrace new and different patterns of thinking.
- Counsel you in business realities and strategies.
- Support you in meetings and presentations.
- Provide guidance during periods of transitions, such as in mergers, acquisitions, new business or product launches, business expansions, or downsizings.
- Allay your fears in making decisions that are risky by coaching you about the notion of increasing your own risk tolerance.

What can you do to maximize the benefits of your relationship with your mentor? The following are some guidelines to help you make it all worthwhile and meet your expectations of the arrangement:

- Seek constructive criticism in a supportive way.
- Ask to be led through a problem-solving process.
- Seek anecdotes and examples of how they succeeded and failed.
- Ask to be introduced to other business associates and other mentors.
- Solicit regular and timely feedback.
- Be prepared for your meeting with your mentor.
- Establish priorities for your agenda.
- Establish guidelines for contact—i.e., no home phone calls, and so on.
- Enhance the mentor's experience and show your appreciation.
- Diplomatically tell the mentor if you disagree with her opinion or counsel and when you feel you might not be learning.

In leveraging your mentor relationships, you don't want to become a political animal and place personal ambition over team and corporate goals and values. The program is for your benefit as well as that of the organization. When you step into a leadership role, you'll want to pass along the favor and become a mentor yourself. Remember, leaders without followers can't be leaders!

One final word on mentoring. None of us is superhuman—we can all use support in our career, if not today, then sometime in the future. Mentoring acknowledges that you do not expect perfection of yourself. Leave your ego out of the equation. These discussions may reveal some aspects about your demeanor that are not positive and need to be addressed to move your career forward. And you may not even be aware of them. So remember, what you gain from a mentoring relationship can increase your marketplace value to its maximum potential and strengthen your competitive advantage as well as that of your company.

———

Secret: It's elementary . . . remember the golden rule: "Do unto others as you would have them do unto you." In the circle of life, behaving stupidly is death to your career. Don't ever burn a bridge.

Conclusion

Well, there you have it—pearls of wisdom from the inner sanctum of the executive search profession that few in the industry will share and that I have earmarked as the most critical during the past 15 years since I have been a recruiter! Of course there are many, many more thoughts in my mind that address broader career issues and hiring topics than just the ones I have included here. However, what I have conveyed in this book are some of the most important weapons that I can add to your career arsenal as you embark upon your navigation adventure (and they also answer questions for those of you who are further along in your pursuits and wonder what career paths should really be like given the fact that none of us is ever educated about how to approach our professional lives).

The reality of it all is that I truly believe every professional deserves the opportunity to navigate a great career, whether you are at the beginning stages of your profession or near the end and are still on the hunt for the next greatest challenge in the corporate world. In addition, I also believe that every hiring executive and hiring corporation deserves the luxury of a competent, thorough, and successful search experience to identify, attract, and hire exceptional talent. After all, without exceptional talent, these corporations would not survive!

No matter how seemingly steep the hurdle or how seemingly huge the obstacle, strive for a goal that is beyond the stars. Whether you are the professional seeking a new chapter in your career or the hiring executive on the hunt for the ideal candidate who will exceed your management team's expectations, go for broke—to use a sports analogy, hit it out of the park!

What I will leave you with is the best, most wisdom-filled "secret" I can relate and one that has been a guiding force for my entire career. It is something that my entrepreneurial father, who was a professional boxer in the early days of the sport, used to share with me: No matter what job you have (and what he really meant was, whether you like the job or not), strive to achieve beyond the top rung of the ladder to an imaginary height that no one else will even *think* of reaching; don't look over your shoulder and worry about what the other person (or company/competition) is doing because you will be losing the time, energy, and speed that you need to achieve what you want to achieve.

You have only once chance to navigate your life both personally and professionally—take these secrets and elements of wisdom and soar!

Bibliography and Other Resources

Books and Articles

Boyle, H. Perry Jr., Benjamin Koby, and Lynn A. Summer. *E*Cruiting: From Job Boards to MetaMarkets—A White Paper on the Internet Recruiting Industry*. San Francisco: Thomas Weisel Partners, LLC, 1999, p. 45.

Hunt, Christopher W. and Scott A. Scanlon, eds. *Navigating Your Career*. New York: John Wiley & Sons, 1998, pp. 15–21.

———. *Executive Recruiters of North America*. Stamford, CT: Hunt-Scanlon, 2000.

Okrent, Daniel. *Twilight of the Boomers. Time*, June 12, 2000, pp. 68–72.

Peters, Tom. *What Will We Do for Work? Time*, May 22, 2000, pp. 68–71.

Silverman, Rachel Emma. "Recruiters' Hunt for Resumes Is Nocturnal Game." *The Wall Street Journal*, September 20, 2000, pp. B1, B4.

Wasserman, Elizabeth. "The New Pay Paradigm: 21st Annual Salary Survey." *Working Woman*, July/August 2000, pp. 57–70.

Company Web Sites

Headhunter.net : www.headhunter.net
Hunt-Scanlon Publishers: www.hunt-scanlon.com
IBN: www.interbiznet.com
Kennedy Information LLC: www.kennedyinfo.com
Korn/Ferry International/FutureStep: www.futurestep.com
Landor Associates: www.landor.com
Monster.com/TMP Worldwide: www.monster.com
ResumeZapper: www.resumezapper.com

Index

Index